Language and Law in Professional Discourse

Language and Law in Professional Discourse: Issues and Perspectives

Edited by

Vijay K. Bhatia, Giuliana Garzone, Rita Salvi, Girolamo Tessuto and Christopher Williams

CAMBRIDGE SCHOLARS PUBLISHING

Language and Law in Professional Discourse: Issues and Perspectives,
Edited by Vijay K. Bhatia, Giuliana Garzone, Rita Salvi,
Girolamo Tessuto and Christopher Williams

This book first published 2014

Cambridge Scholars Publishing

12 Back Chapman Street, Newcastle upon Tyne, NE6 2XX, UK

British Library Cataloguing in Publication Data
A catalogue record for this book is available from the British Library

ISBN (10): 1-4438-5505-7, ISBN (13): 978-1-4438-5505-1

TABLE OF CONTENTS

Part II: Issues of Authority, Power and Identity

LIST OF TABLES

LIST OF FIGURES

ACKNOWLEDGEMENTS

The editors of this volume would like to take this opportunity to thank all the participants in the present book who helped to make the Conference Law, Language and Professional Practice a fruitful forum for scholarly discussion, and who added to the development of knowledge in this field by their valuable contributions included in the present volume.

We would also like to express our deepest thanks to Stephen J. Spedding (Department of Law, University of Naples 2) for all his hard work in collecting and checking sources as well as carrying out technical and language editing for this publication.

In addition, we are grateful to the staff at Cambridge Scholars Publishing for recognizing the value of the contributions included in this volume and for making this publication possible.

INTRODUCTION

VIJAY K. BHATIA, GIULIANA GARZONE, RITA SALVI, GIROLAMO TESSUTO AND CHRISTOPHER WILLIAMS

Language in law has long been the focus of attention from scholars of various persuasions, including legal experts, philosophers, sociologists, and applied linguists, especially discourse and genre analysts. In order to understand how legal professionals participate in their day-to-day activity, it is not enough to focus on language alone, but to study critically how language is used and exploited in everyday professional discourse.

In keeping with the performance of professional activities through language, this edited volume *Language and Law in Professional Practice - Issues and Perspectives* brings together international scholars from within applied linguistics to examine the ways in which the complex and diverse issues of Language and Law play themselves out in discursive and professional genres. Specifically, this volume is the end-product of the 2nd International Conference 'Law, Language and Professional Practice' held at the Department of Law of the Seconda Università degli Studi di Napoli (10-12 May 2012), where keynote lectures and several papers revolved around the central theme. As such, the volume is a carefully selected collection of research papers presented by such scholars and reshaped into chapters after a blind-review process. The volume shares its roots with other selected, peer-reviewed papers from the same Conference published in the volume *Language and Law in Academic and Professional Settings - Analyses and Applications* of the *Explorations in Language and Law* international series (Novalogos, 1/2013). Both editorial sites thus encourage a wider overview of the state-of-the-art description of the existing issues of language and law in professional practice debated at the Conference.

The nine chapters in this volume are organised into two Parts addressing topic areas of legal discourse (written and spoken) relevant to professional practice and communication, namely:

- issues related to the construction, use and accessibility of legislative, judicial and web-mediated discourse; and
- those related to authority, power and identity.

Analyses of such issues from professional and other institutional contexts rely on specific perspectives, varied applications, and different methodological procedures necessary to provide a multifaceted overview of the ongoing research. The book therefore offers a variety of interests in undertaking analyses of legal discourse and genre constructed, interpreted and used within the socially-informed framework of Language and Law.

Part One of the book opens with four studies in topic areas where **Construction, use and accessibility of legislative, judicial and web-mediated discourse** are dealt with.

In the first chapter, 'Facing the *facts*: evaluative patterns in English and Italian judicial language', STANISŁAW GOŹDŹ-ROSZKOWSKI and GIANLUCA PONTRANDOLFO set their analysis in the context of evaluation in legal argumentation in that evaluation reflects the value system(s) espoused by legal systems, cultures, and their respective judicial institutions. Surprisingly, the author argue, research into evaluation of judicial discourse appears as yet to be in its infancy, especially with regard to contrastive cross-language studies. Against this backdrop, their study begins to address this issue by focusing on the most frequent phraseologies co-occurring with the "N *that*" lexico-grammar pattern, and particularly, the most frequent noun "fact" and its Italian equivalent "fatto". Supported by substantial bilingual data, their study reports on the evaluative patterns (understood here as combining both attitudinal and modality meanings) in which "fact *that*"/ "fatto *che*" tend to be used in criminal judgments delivered by the US Supreme Court and Italy's Corte Suprema di Cassazione. The argument is therefore made for both US and Italian judgments to show a clear preference for the use of *fact/fatto* which conveys different types of evaluative meanings. More specifically, *fact that/fatto che*, when used in subject clause-initial position, co-selects negative polarity. As the authors argue, however, polarity is relatively seldom used to convey explicit evaluative (attitudinal) meanings. Instead, both US and Italian judges tend to employ *fact that/fatto che*-related phraseologies for more "covert", i.e. implicit, evaluation to relate to their outcomes, problems, solutions or conclusions.

In the second chapter, 'Drafting court judgment in Italy: history, complexity and simplification', STEFANO ONDELLI presents the results of a research project on court judgments as a genre. The first two stages of his research adopt a qualitative approach and focus on verb tense distribution to account for the generic structure of Italian court judgments. In doing so, the author offers insights into the historical development of specific verb tense patterns and highlights the need for rationalisation and simplification of the generic product. The third stage also includes quantitative research: four corpora in electronic format are compiled, including the Italian version of texts produced by the Court of Justice of the European Union, the Italian Court of Cassation, the Swiss Federal Court, and the Appeal Court of Canton Ticino. The author uses statistical software to assess differences in terms of lexical richness, lexical density and readability, and to calculate verb tense frequencies and distribution patterns. The author argues that shortcomings of automatic quantitative analysis may be redressed through qualitative surveys and, in addition to highlighting differences in the Italian written in Italy, Switzerland and the EU institutions, data can provide insights and suggestions for more effective drafting techniques.

In chapter three, 'Self-construction of legislative discourse through mashups; a multi-perspective analysis', ANNA FRANCA PLASTINA starts from the premise that non-specialist readers often resort to simplified legislative texts in order to gain an understanding of the underlying obscure, ambiguous and complex discourse. However, this solution inevitably brings changes which may alter the meaning and/or structure of the original text. In her study, therefore, the author proposes a pragmatic alternative to simplification by exploring the potential of multimedia technologies which are now permeating law practice. In the current digital age of *visual jurisprudence*, the author admits, particular technological applications may offer new support to the non-specialist community, whose problem of comprehending legislative discourse still remains largely unsolved. As one specific type of web-based applications, therefore, mashups are considered by the author for their possible functional use as non-linear rhetorical easification devices. For this purpose, three Bills originating in the House of Representatives are selected for their importance in reflecting the law-making process of social issues which directly affect lay-people. In this case, mashed-up texts are generated for the corpus of materials in a specialised mashup dealing with US Bills. These new texts are therefore subjected to qualitative, descriptive and multi-perspective analysis. This analysis sheds light on how different semiotic resources and mashup affordances may contribute significantly to reducing information load, clarifying cognitive structuring, and minimising language complexity in all the multi-perspective spaces of discourse.

The chapter 'Expert to layman communication: legal information and advice on the Internet' by JUDITH TURNBULL closes this section. The author focuses on expert-lay communication and specifically on a British government website, direct.gov.uk, which provides information to lay readers about the law and their rights. As an explanation for her study, the author sets forth beforehand that many people nowadays turn to the Internet for specialised information rather than seeking immediate expert advice. Yet, the syntactic complexity and highly technical vocabulary peculiar to the language of the law is one which accentuates the already asymmetrical nature of the expert-lay relationship. With this in mind, the author investigates the ways and the extent to which legal information on divorce matters is 'translated' into comprehensible language on the website. The author's study draws on a number of approaches, both quantitative and qualitative, though primarily Discourse Analysis and Critical Discourse Analysis, in order to capture the complexity of the communicative event. Findings show that the information conveyed by the website is simplified structurally, lexically and syntactically and therefore made more accessible to its very heterogeneous audience, whilst a personal and informal style appears to narrow the gap between expert and lay people. However, the argument is also made about text simplification tending to reduce the complexity of the information within discourse elements and practice, and therefore to possibly mislead the reader into believing that divorce procedure is much simpler than it actually is.

Part Two of this volume addresses **Issues of Authority, Power and Identity**.

In chapter five, 'Competing discourses of respect in a Young Offenders Institution Education Department', PAOLA BOCALE explores the discourses of respect in a Young Offenders Institution in England. With the aim of developing a deeper understanding of perspectives on respect in custodial education, the author examines self-narratives elicited from a prison officer, a library assistant and a teacher working in the Education Department. From the analysis of the different discourses of respect identified in the narratives, respect emerges as a complex of multilayered and interconnecting phenomena which affect both the personal and social dimension of human life. On a personal level, the author argues, respect involves an acknowledgement of a person's individuality and the possibility of having a personal involvement with that individual. Whereas the civilian staff emphasise that respect involves interaction and mutual understanding, the officer's talk is shaped by an authoritarian discourse not defined by an engagement with individual selves but only with the prison institution. The only possible form of respect emerging from the point of view of the officer towards the prisoners is respect as obedience, which depends on how prisoners respond to the condition of being incarcerated without fighting the system. The participants' narratives also provide some insights into the social dimension of respect, such as the contextual factors affecting its perception and recognition in a YOI, including the audience and the power relationship existing between the parties.

In chapter six, 'Constructing authority in international investment arbitration: insights from separate opinions at ICSID', RUTH BREEZE moves into the analytical foreground by attending to the growing evidence that arbitration, which was initially conceived of as a more flexible alternative to standard legal procedures such as litigation, is now developing a body of case law of its own. In this context, the author considers the case of the International Centre for the Settlement of Investment Disputes (ICSID), which resolves major disputes that arise between companies and states. The author relies on some evidence that a body of case law is developing within the ICSID itself, and that arbitrators are increasingly referring to previous awards as precedents when they present their arguments and draft the final Award. Thus, her study looks into the evidence from dissenting opinions published alongside the ICSID Award. These opinions contain many references to previous arbitral decisions, from both ICSID and other international courts of arbitration. Discourse analysis of the referencing systems used in the text shows that arbitrators make use of authoritative figures and previous arbitral decisions to underpin and strengthen their own position, and to bring arguments to a close. In short, this study provides some evidence that previous arbitral decisions are increasingly being used in this context much in the way that precedents would be used in common law pleadings or judgments.

In chapter seven, 'A question of training: issues of language and power in formal police investigative interviews', BRONWEN HUGHES and ANTONELLA NAPOLITANO focus on the analysis of questions and answers in advanced suspect interviews for Tier 3 (Specialist Suspect Interviewers) carried out at the Metropolitan Police Crime Academy in the United Kingdom as part of formal police training. The interviews (cognitive PACE evidentiary interviews) are investigated through the Conversation Analysis approach to "institutional talk", with particular attention to the structure of the dyadic, asymmetrical formal interview, the pre-allocation of turns, question typology and third turn receipt markers. After a brief overview of the procedural models which govern interviewing techniques (*Enhanced Cognitive Interview* (ECI), *TEDS* (*tell*, *explain*, *describ*e, *show*) framework), the authors begin with an investigation of suspect-initiated questions among which the authors identify three distinct groups: requests for clarification, polemic enquiries and information-seeking questions. A second section is devoted to the interviewing officer's third turn receipt markers, such as neutral "ok" and formulations with lexical variation. A further section of their study analyses the elicitation/information-seeking questions put forward by the interviewing officers and posits that such officers are not always able to adhere to the *TEDS* framework which encourages open, non-threatening questions, but regularly adopt more traditional "wh" questions, thus narrowing the suspect's scope for response. Finally, the authors illustrate that conversationalisation techniques are recurrently employed throughout the interviews, though such 'democratized' discourse would invariably appear to serve goal-oriented institutional aims.

In chapter eight, 'A respected neutral expert – arbitrator profile in focus', TARJA SALMI-TOLONEN discusses the arbitrator's construction of identity through narratives. The author's premise is that in Europe, as in the rest of the world, arbitration has become more and more common as a mechanism for the settling of commercial disputes. She goes on to state that one attraction arbitration has is that the companies in dispute can choose the arbitrators themselves. The qualities the companies appreciate in arbitrators are their professional qualifications and experience and – more importantly – the personality of the arbitrator. Therefore, arbitrators' identities are focused upon. By looking into arbitrators' interviews, the author examines how a sense of self or an identity is conveyed and indexed, and seeks to identify what their fundamental assumptions and concerns are, what lexicons are used in their tales, and whether their usual way of interacting can be found and whether a common arbitrator profile can be constructed. The author's approach is therefore eclectic, combining narrative analysis, recontextualisation theory and appropriation theory. Findings suggest that both shared and individual qualifications account for three distinct profiles: that of an authority, a healer, and an administrator.

VIEIRA TORRES AMITZA closes Part II with her study 'Role hybridity in professional practice in a hearing in the Special Criminal Court'. The author uses the qualitative approach to interpretive research in order to analyse the interaction data in real speech. In analysing the communicative intent of the speakers in the production of their utterances, the author discusses discourse hybridity in professional contexts where the judge's role emerges from a Hearing in the Special Criminal Court in Brazil. The latter represents a legal setting where criminal contraventions and misdemeanours are tried and punished by an imprisonment not exceeding two years. Specifically, therefore, the author aims: (1) to describe the hybridity roles played by the judge in a hearing in the Special Criminal Court; (2) to investigate the reasons why certain roles are constructed in this talk-in-interaction; and (3) to identify which roles are deliberately played and which ones are imposed by virtue of the specific institutional mandate in a Criminal Hearing. As a result, the author identifies two main role-sets: professional roles, referring to the accomplishment of the institutional mandate of the Hearing, and pedagogic roles, marked by an orientation to the parties.

As has become increasingly clear throughout this contents overview, the research landscape offered by contributors covers diverse and complex features of legal discourse construction where socially informed aspects of language use are inherently negotiated by professional practices. Such features thus provide the wide scope for the critical study of legal language as a tool for social action, and set up a descriptive and interpretive framework for engaging with representations of legal discourses and genres where authority, power and ideology are established and communicated as part of the socio-cultural contexts of those who use language. Formation of specific discursive practices within professional, institutional and organisational legal frameworks is no less relevant to acknowledge theoretically canvassed areas of hybridity, intertextuality, interdiscursivity and recontextualisation in legal language and discourse. By providing different thematic contents and distinctive arguments, this book will therefore offer both a resource and a stimulus to its readers.

PART I:

CONSTRUCTION, USE AND ACCESSIBILITY OF LEGISLATIVE AND (EXTRA) JUDICIAL DISCOURSE

CHAPTER ONE

FACING THE *FACTS*: EVALUATIVE PATTERNS IN ENGLISH AND ITALIAN JUDICIAL LANGUAGE[1]

STANISLAW GOŹDŹ-ROSZKOWSKI
AND GIANLUCA PONTRANDOLFO

Introduction

Attitudes, value judgements, or assessments represent a crucial aspect of judicial language. Assessing the status of evidence and the applicability of the relevant law requires an ability to discriminate among a number of epistemic distinctions. Apart from making decisions, judges are expected to justify them by referring to a received body of law and observing the principle of neutrality. Judicial activity routinely includes interpreting statutes, various legal documents and earlier court decisions. In the case of appellate courts, a substantial part of judicial argumentation involves expressing agreement or disagreement with decisions given by lower courts, opinions expressed by counsel representing the parties, as well as opinions arrived at by fellow judges from the same bench. Judicial opinions should be free of any overt expressions of personal stance and at the same time judges are under pressure to speak with a definitive voice (Solan 1993: 2). There is little doubt that judicial opinions represent a fascinating area to examine the way(s) in which this professional community employs various linguistic mechanisms to express a range of evaluative functions.

There is a long and rich research tradition of studying the linguistic mechanisms employed by speakers and writers to convey their personal

[1] This chapter stems from the ideas of both authors on the subject matter. Sections 1 and 2 were written by Stanisław Goźdź-Roszkowski, sections 3 and 4 by Gianluca Pontrandolfo.

feelings and value judgements. Many different conceptual and theoretical approaches are reflected in a wide range of terminology, including *appraisal* (e.g. Martin / White 2005), *stance* (e.g. Biber 2006), *metadiscourse* (e.g. Hyland / Tse 2004), *modality* (e.g. Palmer 1987), *sentiment* (e.g. Taboada / Grieve 2004), *evaluative*, *attitudinal* or *affective* language (e.g. Ochs 1989), *evidentiality* (e.g. Chafe / Nichols 1986) and *evaluation* (e.g. Hunston 1994, 2011).

Surprisingly, linguistic research into this phenomenon as it applies to legal language is still in its infancy. One strand of legal linguistics research on evaluative meanings is linked to the relationship between testimonial evidence and subjective judgements of witnesses providing such evidence (Heffer 2007). Another line of research concerns the study of legal argumentation (cf. Mazzi 2007, 2010).

More recently, Goźdź-Roszkowski / Pontrandolfo (forthcoming) document the use and functions of frequent evaluative patterns by comparing the "N that" pattern (nouns followed by an appositive *that*-clause) in American and Italian criminal judgments. The study demonstrates the central importance of evaluation for legal argumentation and the crucial link between evaluation and phraseology. More specifically, it applies the new concept of recurrent semantic sequences (Hunston 2008) manifested in the "N *that*" pattern to explore the linguistic construal of evaluation by judges. It is argued that judicial opinions exhibit a significant correlation between the frequent occurrence of abstract nouns belonging to the semantically defined category of "argumentation" (such as *argument*, *assumption*, *fact*, *claim*, etc.) followed by appositive *that*-clauses and co-occurring with linguistically varied items expressing evaluative meaning. These linguistically varied items range from adjectives (e.g. *dubious*, *unavailing*, *compelling*, etc.), and verbs (e.g. *rejected*, *commend*, *disapproved*, etc.), to adverbs (e.g. *inexorably*) and their presence in such a syntactically constrained environment illustrates another claim that evaluation is to a great extent contextual and cumulative, i.e. evaluative meaning is spread across phraseologies rather than attached to individual words. Finally, evaluative meanings are not always immediately conspicuous: a great deal of phraseology with appositive *that*-clause qualifiers patterns shows "latent patterning", i.e. patterning in language that is not obvious to intuition or to language as it is observed in single texts (Sinclair / Coulthard 1975). Apart from overtly and explicitly evaluative items (nouns like *omission*, *problem*; verbs such as *disagree*, *agree*; adjectives as *illogical*, *logical*, *correct*; adverbs like *wrongly*, *correctly*, etc.), there are a whole range of nouns that pass unnoticed because they are connoted in a less explicit way. There is nothing intrinsically positive or negative in nouns like *fact*, *argument*, *conclusion*, *view* or *fatto*, *conclusione*, *valutazione*, *tesi*, when viewed in isolation as discrete items, and yet these status nouns are employed by judges in contexts marked by strong positive or negative polarities.

The present study extends the findings provided in Goźdź-Roszkowski and Pontrandolfo (forthcoming) by focusing on the most frequent noun in the "N that" pattern in both American and Italian texts, i.e. "fact *that*"/"fatto *che*" and exploring its role in the construal of epistemic stance in American and Italian judicial language. The importance of *fact* as an epistemic noun is recognised in the literature (e.g. Biber et al. 1999: 648-651). The widespread use of "fact" with *that*- clauses to express epistemic stance across different academic disciplines is also documented in Biber's corpus-based study of spoken and written university registers (2006: 112). Hunston (2008, 2011) reports the high occurrences of "fact *that*" not only in law, but also in the disciplinary discourses of politics, education, humanities and social sciences. *Fact* seems to differ from other status nouns, such as *assumption* or *hypothesis* because of the more general and abstract difficulty inherent in the nature of facts and reality. As Hunston (2011) points out, propositions can have factual status without actually being referred to as "fact". Conversely, using the label *fact* does not always correspond to the same "factual" evaluation of a given proposition by a particular discourse community. There is some evidence (coming mostly from the Academic sections of the British National Corpus and discussed in Hunston 2011) that the use of epistemic status of *fact* may vary depending on a given discipline. For example, disciplines belonging to the natural sciences, engineering or medicine contain considerably fewer instances of *fact* to label their propositions than disciplines grouped as humanities, the disciplines of politics, law and education (Hunston 2011). The statistical data might come as a surprise since the natural sciences or engineering are popularly considered as hard sciences with a more direct alignment between proposition and the world than is the case with "soft" sciences such as humanities, law or politics.

The present study aims to document how *fact* tends to be used in the domain of law by the discourse community of judges. It focuses on judgments handed down by the *United States Supreme Court* and Italy's *Corte Suprema di Cassazione* because of their central importance for the judicial systems in both jurisdictions and their law-making function. The opinions of the Supreme Court judges are considered by legal communities as one of the most striking examples of "living law" or *law in action* to refer to the pioneer paper by the distinguished legal scholar Roscoe Pound (1910), (cf. Cadoppi 1999: 253; Garavelli 2010: 154).

In what follows, the Materials and Method section introduces further clarification of the methodology as well as the composition of the corpus used in our study. In the Results section we provide and discuss the findings of our analysis and in the Conclusions section conclusions and directions envisaged for future research.

Materials and Method

From a methodological point of view, our study is informed by Corpus Linguistics research tradition (cf. Teubert 2005; McEnery / Xiao / Tono 2006) and recent advancements in phraseology (Granger / Meunier 2008; Schulze / Romer 2008). Corpus linguistics methodology is employed by relying on a large and representative collection of electronically-stored judgments given by the Supreme Courts in the United States and Italy. Such corpus material is amenable to standard data-manipulation techniques ranging from the identification of a search word and scrutiny of its immediate linguistic environment (key-word-in-context or concordance lines), through the production of frequency-based word lists to calculating the relative frequency of comparable lexical items in the two sub-corpora. These operations were performed by means of WordSmith Tools (version 5.0), developed by Mike Scott (2008).

The other crucial concept – i.e. phraseology – is understood very broadly as combining and extending the collocational and colligational aspects of co-occurrence in language. In our study, we follow the definition of phraseology proposed recently by Gries:

> the co-occurrence of a form or a lemma of a lexical item and one more or additional linguistic elements of various kinds which functions as one semantic unit in a clause or sentence and whose frequency of co-occurrence is larger than expected on the basis of chance (2008: 6).

In consequence, what counts as a phraseologism must be based on frequency; it can be a multi-word unit and it should be semantically motivated.

In light of the claim that evaluation is contextual and cumulative, this study draws upon Hunston's (2008: 271) concept of "semantic sequences", namely "recurring sequences of words and phrases that may be very diverse in form and which are therefore more usually characterised as sequences of meaning elements rather than as formal sequences" to identify frequent evaluative patterns in the judgments. We focused on semantic sequences comprising the grammar pattern (Francis et al 1996/1998 in Hunston 2008: 278) "N *that*", where N stands for general abstract nouns (or head-nouns (Francis 1993)) belonging to the semantic category of "argumentation" followed by appositive *that*-clauses. It is generally accepted (e.g. Halliday / Matthiessen 2004: 637) that nouns in this pattern are indicative of the epistemic status of the proposition expressed in the *that*-clause and that projected *that*-clauses of this kind are important to disciplinary epistemology.

As far as data are concerned, the present study relies on bilingual comparable corpus data consisting of two sub-corpora: American and Italian, each of approximately 500,000 words. The corpus is both domain and genre-specific in that it includes only criminal cases. This restriction was motivated by our intention to concentrate on a coherent and consistent body of case-law in view of the courts' enormous judicial output. In addition, focusing on a specific legal domain enables the hypothesis of a correlation between a specific field of law (e.g. civil, anti-tort, labour law, etc.) and the type of evaluative patterns involved in these texts to be tested empirically in the near future.

The American sub-corpus data include 51 opinions handed down by the United States Supreme Court totalling 501,024 tokens sampled from the period 1999-2006. The opinions were accessed via FindLaw.com, a well-known legal information web portal. They are part of a large, multi-genre collection known as the *American Law Corpus* (Goźdź-Roszkowski 2011).

The Italian sub-corpus used in this analysis comes from a sub-corpus of the *Corpus of Criminal Judgments* (COSPE; cf. Pontrandolfo 2013: 171-183), named COSPE-Sup. It comprises 134 judgments, all of them delivered by the criminal division of the Italian Supreme Court in the period 2005-2011. It amounts to 502,994 tokens, and it was designed according to two basic criteria: first of all, the subject matter, since all the select judgments deal with criminal cases; secondly, the time span, since it only includes judgments issued between 2005 and 2011. All the judgments were collected from the large case-law section of the online De-Jure database.[2] As regards the drafting of the judgments, although they are the joint result of the opinions of the five or nine judges making up the Court, they were actually drafted by a single judge, the so-called "reporting judge" (*giudice relatore/estensore*), whose function is to explain the main points of the case.

Despite the differences between the Common Law and Continental Civil Law traditions, the Supreme Courts in both the US and Italy share some similarities with respect to their roles and functions. It is generally

[2] http://www.dejure.giuffre.it [accessed on 12/09/2012].

accepted in legal comparative literature that the United States Supreme Court and Italy's *Corte Suprema di Cassazione* can be deemed directly comparable (cf. Cappelletti et al. 1989: 142).

Results

In this section, we present our corpus findings regarding a particular structure, namely "fact *that*"/"fatto *che*", which is the most frequent "N that" pattern in both sub-corpora, against the backdrop of the appositive *that*-clauses (Francis 1993, 1994; Hunston 2008, 2011).

As mentioned in the previous section, we queried our corpus for the "N that" pattern with the aim of looking at the frequency and function of individual nouns in this specific syntactic structure. By looking at the lexical (collocations) and grammatical (colligations) environments in which the head-nouns appeared, we analysed recurring semantic sequences (Hunston 2008; 2011) in judicial discourse, observing the phraseological constraints that characterised some head-nouns[3] in relation to positive/neutral or negative polarity.

A thorough discussion of the whole range of head-nouns followed by evaluative co(n)text is beyond the scope of the present chapter (cf. Goźdź-Roszkowski / Pontrandolfo forthcoming for an in-depth analysis of the "N *that*" pattern). As a matter of fact, the focus of our contrastive study is the most frequent and contentious (Hunston 2011: 108) "general" noun, to follow the above-mentioned labels of Francis, namely *fact*. In this way we took up Francis's challenge of examining appositive *that*-clauses believing that this could profitably lead to "an exploration of the grammar of some of the most frequent noun-heads, of which *fact* and *reason*, for example, promise rich findings" (1993: 155).

First and foremost, we decided to analyse this "N *that*" pattern from a syntactic point of view with the aim of gaining a clearer picture of the phraseological framework in which it operates. To do so, we examined three basic syntactic situations:

a) "fact *that*" as **subject or the clause**;

(1) *The fact that* […] has no logical bearing on the analysis

[3] In this study, we use the term "head-noun" as a way to refer to the noun to which the appositive clause is attached. The nouns in this construction are usually unspecific and require lexical realisation in its immediate context to be properly understood. We adopted this definition as a criterion our nouns had to meet in order to be considered relevant for the current analysis.

(2) È stato poi ritenuto decisivo *il fatto che* fossero trascorsi tre anni dal fatto.

[*The fact that* three years had passed since the event has been considered crucial]

b) "fact *that*" as **object of the clause;**[4]

(3) The argument is flawed. It ignores *the fact that* only relatively recently have the penalty and guilt phases been conducted separately.

(4) La Corte [...] ha valorizzato *il fatto che* [...]
[The Court [...] enhanced *the fact that* [...]]

c) "fact *that*" **preceded by prepositions** and therefore used as subordinate clauses, such as causal, concessive, final, etc.;

(5) The dictum may be attributable *to the fact that* the cases recognizing a defendant's evidentiary rights and the prosecution's duty to prove all elements beyond a reasonable doubt were still decades away.

(6) Siffatta lettura della norma in esame non risulterebbe ostacolata *dal fatto che* essa riproduce parzialmente il testo dell'art. [...]

[This reading of the norm would not be hindered *by the fact that* it partially reproduces the text of Art. [...]]

The quantitative analysis of both sub-corpora revealed interesting similar behaviours in the way the nominal pattern "fact *that*" is used in US and IT criminal judgments, as can be seen in the following chart.

"Fact *that*" is mostly used with recurring prepositions (43% in the US sub-corpus, 57% in the Italian one), a result which is in line with Hunston (2011: 113), who found that the most frequent three-word phrases having "fact *that*" as core of the semantic sequence included a preposition. As far as the American sub-corpus is concerned, the most frequent prepositions are: *(up)on/by/despite/notwithstanding/of/from/to/for the fact that*. As for the Italian counterpart, the most common prepositions are: *del* [of]/*al* [to]/*dal* [from]/*nel* [in]/*sul* [on] *fatto che*. Frequent prepositions in the corpus are key to an understanding of the fundamental phraseology of the

[4] We excluded from the analysis cases in which "fact that" was embedded into standardised formulae, such as (e.g. for the simple fact that), or cases in which it was used as a "retrospective label" (Francis 1994: 85) (e.g. [...], a fact that it is not in line with). We also excluded the instances where the noun "facts" is the term to describe the section of the judgment (cf. Bhatia 1993: 118-136).

genre (Gledhill 2000: 124), which is why they can be considered "salient items" (Gledhill 2000: 115). Moreover, they play a pivotal role from the syntactic point of view, as they contribute to the construction of different clause-types.

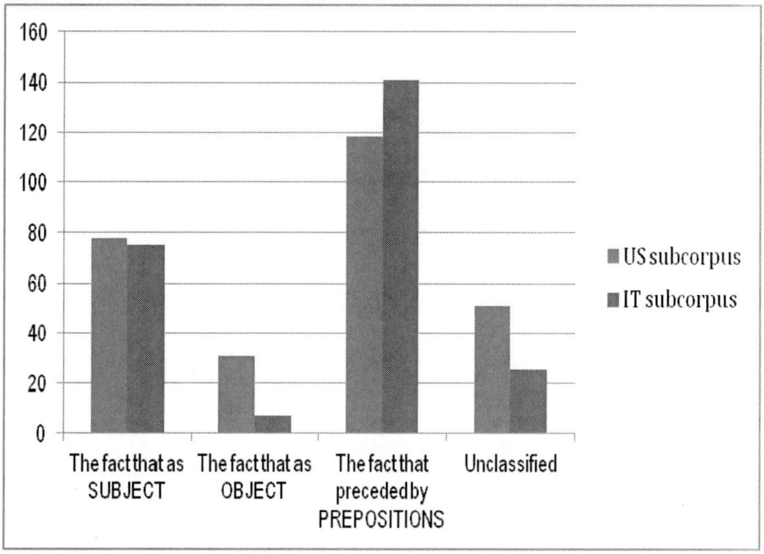

Figure 1-1 "Fact *that*" from a syntactic point of view in the US and IT sub-corpora

"Fact *that*" is also used in a syntactic construction whereby it is the subject (28% in the US sub-corpus and 30% in the IT one) or object (18% in the US sub-corpus, 10% in the Italian one) of the clause. We focus our attention on the former pattern since the latter is not particularly significant for the purposes of the study. We can only notice that it is more frequent in the US sub-corpus, but does not show any distinctive phraseological behaviours.

When used in the first position, as subject of the clause, "fact *that*" co-occurs with negative particles and negativity in general. The same does not necessarily apply when it is the object of the clause.

The following chart shows the semantic polarity of "fact *that*" in the clause-initial position:

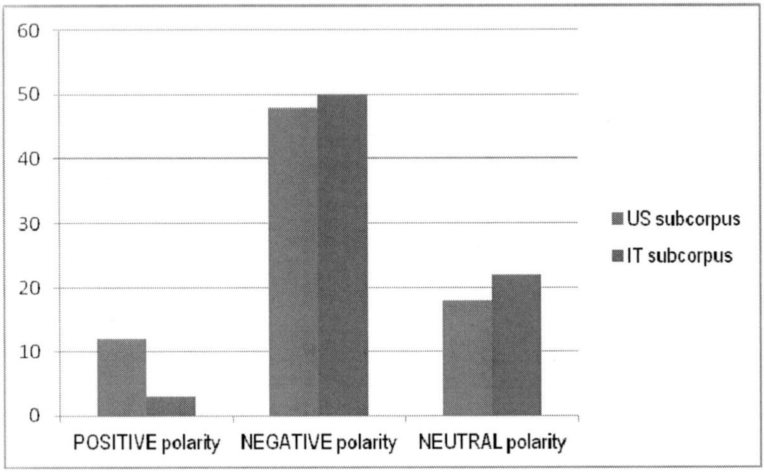

Figure 1-2 Semantic polarities of "fact *that*" in subject position in the US and IT sub-corpora

Both sub-corpora are characterised by negative polarity (US: 62% vs. IT: 67%). Far from being a mere coincidence, there seems to be a consistency in the way evaluative meaning co-occurs with the syntactic positions of our head-noun. It is interesting to note that there are striking similarities in both sub-corpora.

The following tables show the frequent negativity, sometimes explicitly marked, in the US sub-corpus (Table 1-1) as well as in the IT sub-corpus (Table 1-2). The example sentences are truncated to illustrate general co-occurrence trends.

Negativity is mostly phrased through lexico-grammatical devices: the use of the particle *not*/*non*, and therefore through negative sentences, as well as through evaluative connotative items, namely adverbs (e.g. *little* or *poco*/*nulla*), verbs (e.g. *invalidate* or *stridere*), adjectives (e.g. *illogical*/*insufficient* or *scarso*/*irrilevante*) and nouns (e.g. *problems* or *rilievo*).

The fact *that*	(surely) *does not* signify that
	does not mean that
	does not change our view
	does not alter the conclusion/result
	does not necessarily mean
	does not automatically deprive that interpretation of
	does not put it outside the scope of
	does not establish that
	does not overcome the failure
	does not provide basis for
	does not suggest anything suggests that there is *no*
	does not resolve the question
	does not render
	did not make this a difference or dispute of a hypothetical or abstract character.
	was not a sufficient reason
	does not make their claim reviewable
	would not be a rational ground
	would not undermine the public character
	would be *invalidating* if
	has no logical bearing on the analysis
	says *little* about
	poses two related *problems*

Table 1-1 Negative polarity of "fact *that*" in the US sub-corpus (right-hand co(n)text)

Il fatto *che* [The fact *that*]	è *irrilevante* [is *unimportant*] *non* ha rilievo [is *not* important] *poco* rileva [has *little* importance] a *nulla* rileva [*nothing* proves] è *privo* di rilievo [is *not* important] *non* ha molto rilievo [has *no* great importance] di *scarso* rilievo è [has *little* importance]
	prova *poco* (proves *almost nothing*)
	non può, di per sé, giustificare il diniego di [*cannot*, alone, justify the denial of the benefit]
	non comporta il divieto di [*does not* imply the prohibition to]
	non era consentito [*was not* allowed]
	stride con le dichiarazioni degli imputati [*clashes* with the declarations of the defendants]
	non può essere assimilato a [*cannot* be likened to]

Table 1-2 Negative polarity of "fact *that*" in the IT sub-corpus (right-hand co(n)text)

It is interesting to note, from a contrastive perspective, that in the Italian sub-corpus quite often positive polarity is expressed via negative particles, as can be seen in the following examples:

(7) […] *non* poteva portare a valutazione *diversa*
[…] *cannot* lead to a *different* evaluation]

(8) […] *non* configura profili di *nullità*
[…] *does not* set up cases of *nullity*]

(9) […] *non* significava che *non* andava posto rimedio a tale situazione di palese *illegittimità*.
[…] *does not* imply that this clearly *illegitimate* situation *did not* have to be settled]

The use of the double negative is one of the most striking features of Italian legalese and one of the targets of the plain language movement (Ittig and *Academia della Crusca* 2011): the combination of two negative axiological items (*non* + *diversa* in (7), *non* + *nullità* in (8) or *non* + *non* in (9)) affirms the truthfulness of the sentences. In (8), for example, instead of saying "it is valid", the judge prefers to formulate the sentence in convoluted terms, that is "it is not null". One of the possible interpretations of this feature is politeness (Kurzon 2001): the judge is preserving the positive face of the addressee, thus mitigating the effect of his/her evaluation.

In the next stage of our research, following Hunston (2011: 113-116), we decided to focus on the sequences where "fact *that*" is preceded by a preposition – the most frequent patterning in our corpus (cf. Figure 1-1). We therefore categorised each single pattern according to seven groups (cf. Table 1-3). Then, in order to have a clearer picture of the evaluative, epistemic patterns in our corpus, we further grouped our semantic sequences containing "fact *that*" into the three broad "motifs" identified by Groom (2007): the "cause" motif (categories 1-2-3), the "orientation" motif (category 4) and the "human response" motif (categories 5-6-7).

<table>
<tr><th>Hunston's categories (2011)</th><th>Groom's motifs (2007)</th></tr>
<tr><td>1. FACT IS THE BASIS FOR A PRACTICAL OUTCOME OR REASONING

(10) Other courts routinely *rely on* ***the fact that*** a prior statement is given under oath in judicial proceedings

(11) I giudici di merito *hanno ancorato* il loro ragionamento ***al fatto che*** […]
[The lower-court judges *have based* their reasoning *on the fact that…*]</td><td rowspan="3">A. THE "CAUSE" MOTIF</td></tr>
<tr><td>2. FACT EXPLAINS SOMETHING

(12) This dictum may be *attributable to* ***the fact that*** the cases recognizing a defendant's evidentiary rights and the prosecution's duty to prove all elements beyond a reasonable doubt were still decades away.

(13) La genuinità del primitivo ricordo del teste *sarebbe dimostrata* altresì ***dal fatto che*** […]
[The authenticity of the first memory of the witness *would be also demonstrated by the fact that…*]</td></tr>
<tr><td>3. FACT IS THE CAUSE OF A PROBLEM OR ITS SOLUTION

(14) The artificial (and consequently unfair) nature of the resulting sentence *is aggravated by* ***the fact that*** prosecutors must charge all relevant facts about the way the crime was committed before a presentence investigation examines the criminal conduct, perhaps before the trial itself, i.e., before many of the facts relevant to punishment are known.

(15) […] una evidente contraddizione *dovuta* ***al fatto che*** la Corte ha ritenuto […]
[…a clear contradiction *due to the fact that* the Court believed…]</td></tr>
</table>

<table>
<tr><td>4. SOMETHING USES OR ASSUMES A FACT (OR NOT)

(16) Thus, despite the fact that the legislature had passed a law mandating nonpartisan judicial elections, despite the fact that the new law expressly repealed the old law, despite the fact that the Governor had signed the law, and despite the fact that the State had submitted the new law to the United States Attorney General for preclearance under §5, this new law was not operative for one reason:

(17) […] partendo dal fatto che i due imputati sono stati definiti a basso livello intellettivo
[…starting from the fact that the two defendants have been defined as having low intellective capacities]</td><td>B. THE “ORIENTATION” MOTIF</td></tr>
<tr><td>5. BE AWARE OR UNAWARE OF A FACT

(18) We are mindful of the fact that a statute should be read where possible as effecting a “symmetrical and coherent regulatory scheme”.

(19) […] si mostrò consapevole del fatto che il giudice […]
[…he was aware of the fact that the judge…]</td><td rowspan="2">C. THE “HUMAN RESPONSE” MOTIF</td></tr>
<tr><td>6. PEOPLE TALK ABOUT A FACT

(20) In that case, the Court made repeated reference to the fact that its inquiry into whether the military tribunal had jurisdiction to try and punish Milligan turned in large part on the fact that Milligan was not a prisoner of war, but a resident of Indiana arrested while at home there.

(21) La Corte territoriale ha convenuto con la difesa sul fatto che […]

[The territorial Court agreed with the defence on the fact that…]</td></tr>
</table>

7. AFFECTIVE REACTION TO A FACT (22) As to "depravity of mind," the court *held* ***the fact that*** the defendant fired a second shotgun blast into a victim after he was dead *to be insufficient* as a matter of law, see Pritchett, 621 S. W. 2d, at 139 (explaining that the depravity in such an action falls short of that exhibited by the defendant in Godfrey, supra), […] (23) Con il terzo motivo [il ricorrente] *si duole* ***del fatto che*** illegittimamente il Tribunale [With the third reason [the appellant] *complains about the fact that* the Court illegitimately…]	

Table 1-3 Groups of evaluative sequences containing "fact *that*" with examples from the US and IT sub-corpora

The breakdown of the quantitative and qualitative results of the analysis is shown in the following charts:

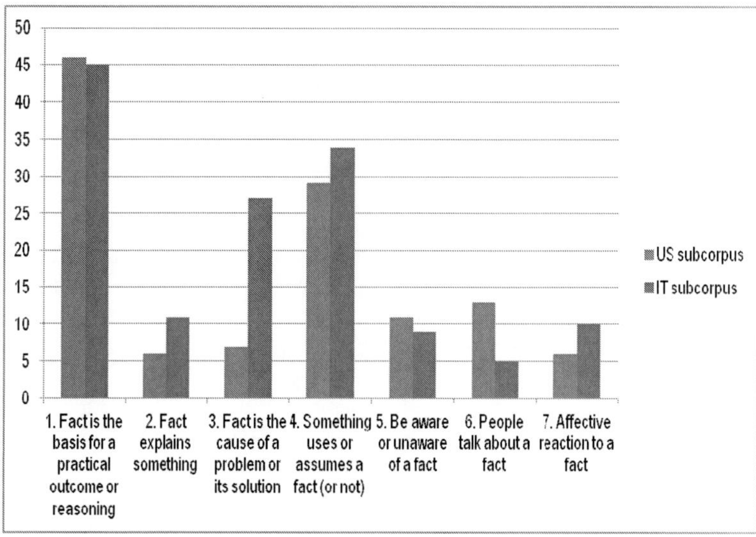

Figure 1-3 Hunston's categories in the US and IT sub-corpora

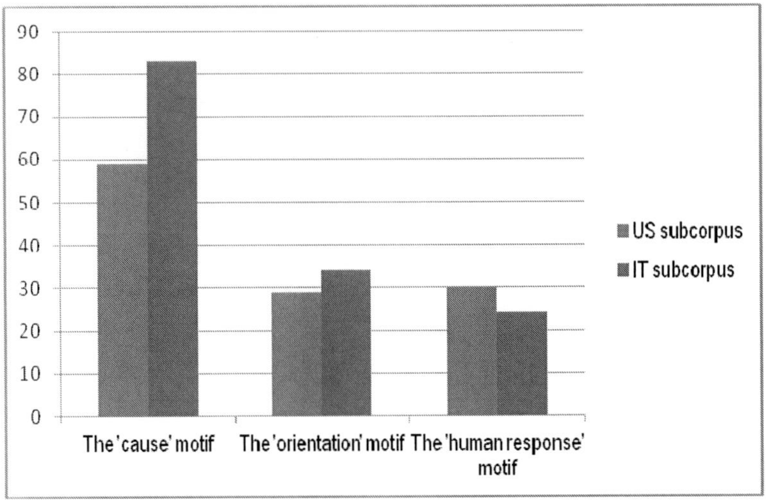

Figure 1-4 Groom's motifs in the US and IT sub-corpora

First of all, the results are very similar in the US and IT sub-corpora, which is indeed a very interesting finding.

"Fact *that*" is mainly used by American and Italian judges to express the cause of things (the "cause" motif accounts for 50% of the US nominal patterns and 59% of the Italian ones), less frequently to express "orientation", that is to say, if facts are ignored or taken into account (25% in the US sub-corpus vs. 24% in the Italian one) and their or others' "response" (25% in the US sub-corpus vs. 17% in the Italian one).

According to these preliminary results, American and Italian judges would tend to refer to facts for their arguments in a more objective way, preferring not to talk so much about their own opinions on facts or those of the other judicial interactants playing a role in the discourse. In this sense, there seems to be a more "covert"/implicit evaluation in the texts than an "overt"/explicit one. As a matter of fact, we hardly encountered cases in which judges explicitly express their opinion, such as "We don't agree with/We agree with/We refuse": propositions seem to be hedged so as to avoid explicitness. In this perspective, facts are for judges a means to get to their outcomes, problems, solutions or conclusions. Judges tend to avoid orientating themselves around facts, talking about them or reacting affectively – either positively or negatively – to them. If we analyse in depth Hunston's 7th category (affective reaction to a fact), we realise that it is full of examples where judges report the defendants' reactions to the case, but not their own judgements on the facts. Reaction is mainly conveyed through mental verbs (Biber et al. 1999: 362-363, 368-369, 370) or illocutive and expositive verbs (Rovere 2000) such as *lamentare/complain*, *tranquillizzare/reassure*, etc. (as shown in example 23).

Conclusions

The present chapter, by no means exhaustive, is an attempt to demonstrate the empirical importance of evaluative patterns in judicial discourse. A case study on the most frequent head-noun in our corpus, "fact", in the semantic pattern "N *that*", opened up interesting perspectives on the way evaluation is embedded in criminal judgments. The combination of close attention to individual instances and interpretations of large quantities of data proved to be useful, bringing novel insights into how evaluative language works (Hunston 2011: 65).

From a contrastive point of view, and in spite of the inevitable cultural and judicial differences between the United States and Italy which belong respectively to Common and Civil law traditions, judges seem to express evaluation in a very similar way, at least according to these preliminary findings on the specific key noun *fact*.

Latent patterning proved to play a pivotal role in the evaluation process. As a matter of fact, the quantitative and qualitative analyses carried out in this study revealed that many co(n)texts of the "fact" are covertly evaluative. We can interpret this finding on account of two opposing forces interacting in the opinion drafting process: on the one hand, judges are expected to draft linear texts where the formulation of the decision merely reflects the application of relevant legal norms to the facts of the case (cf. Mazzi 2010: 374, Garavelli 2010: 97); on the other hand, the articulation of the judges' argumentation presupposes a certain degree of subjectivity and therefore evaluative stances. The investigation of the appositive *that*-clauses following "facts" allowed us to discover these (covert) evaluative patterns in judicial discourse.

Through the corpus-based investigation of "fact *that*" we also discovered syntactic preferences encoded in judicial discourse. The "N *that*" pattern was basically used as bait to bring to light judges' evaluation. Although certain head-nouns, such as *fact*, can be termed "attitudinally neutral" (Francis 1994: 93), they can easily take on "positive" or "negative" meanings in discourse, according to the lexical environment in which they are used, as we demonstrated in the previous section.

We believe that this is part of the "legal grammar" of the judges, stylistic conventions rooted in time by usage which have become part of the judges' discourse strategies and should be considered when analysing judicial language.

References

Bhatia, Vijay K. 1993. *Analysing Genre: Language Use in Professional Settings*. Harlow: Longman.

Biber, Douglas / Conrad, Susan / Finegan, Edward / Johansson, Stig / Leech, Geoffrey 1999. *Longman Grammar of Spoken and Written English*. Harlow: Pearson Education Limited.

Biber, Douglas 2006. *University Language. A Corpus-based Study of Spoken and Written Language.* Amsterdam/Philadelphia: John Benjamins.

Cadoppi, Alberto 1999. *Il valore del precedente nel diritto penale. Uno studio sulla dimensione in action della legalità*. Torino: Giappichelli.

Cappelletti, Mario / Kollmer, Paul J. / Olson, Joanne M. 1989. *The Judicial Process in Comparative Perspective*. Oxford/New York: Clarendon.

Chafe, Wallace / Nichols, Johanna (eds.) 1986. *Evidentiality: The Linguistic Encoding of Epistemology*. Norwood, NJ: Ablex.

Francis, Gill 1993. A corpus-driven approach to grammar. Principles, methods and examples. In Baker, M. / Francis, G. / Tognini-Bonelli, E. (eds.) *Text and Technology. In Honour of John Sinclair*. Amsterdam/Philadelphia: John Benjamins: 137-156.

—. 1994. Labelling discourse: an aspect of nominal-group lexical cohesion. In Coulthard, M. (ed.) *Advances in Written Text Analysis*. London/New York: Routledge: 83-101.

Francis, Gill / Hunston, Susan / Manning, Elizabeth 1996. *Collins Cobuild Grammar Patterns 1: Verbs.* London: HarperCollins.

—. 1998. *Collins Cobuild Grammar Patterns 2: Nouns and Adjectives.* London: HarperCollins.

Garavelli, Mario 2010. I giudici e il linguaggio. In Visconti, J. (ed.) *Lingua e Diritto. Livelli di analisi*. Milano: LED.

Gledhill, Christopher 2000. The discourse function of collocation in research article introductions. *English for Specific Purposes* 19: 115-135.

Goźdź-Roszkowski, Stanislaw 2011. *Patterns of Linguistic Variation in American Legal English. A Corpus-Based Study*. Frankfurt: Peter Lang.

Goźdź-Roszkowski, Stanislaw / Pontrandolfo, Gianluca Forthcoming 2014. Evaluative patterns in judicial discourse: a corpus-based phraseological perspective on American and Italian criminal judgments. *Research in Language* 12(1) March 2014.

Granger, Sylviane / Meunier, Fanny 2008. *Phraseology: An Interdisciplinary Perspective* Amsterdam/Philadelphia: John Benjamins.

Gries, Stefan Th. 2008. Phraseology and linguistic theory: a brief survey. In Granger, S. / Meunier, F. (eds.) *Phraseology: An Interdisciplinary Perspective* Amsterdam/Philadelphia: John Benjamins: 3-25.

Groom, Nicholas 2007. Phraseology and epistemology in Humanities writing. Unpublished PhD thesis, University of Birmingham.

Halliday, Michael A.K. / Matthiessen, Christian 2004. *An Introduction to Functional Grammar* (3rd ed.). London: Arnold.

Heffer, Chris 2007. Judgement in Court: evaluating participants in courtroom discourse. In Kredens, K. / Goźdź-Roszkowski, S. (eds.) *Language and the Law: International Outlooks. Lodz Studies in Language series*, vol. 16. Frankfurt: Peter Lang: 145-179.

Hunston, Susan 1994. Evaluation and organisation in academic discourse. In Coulthard, M. (ed.) *Advances in Written Text Analysis*. London: Routledge: 191-218.

—. 2008. Starting with the small words: patterns, lexis and semantic sequences. In *International Journal of Corpus Linguistics* 13(3), Amsterdam/Philadelphia: John Benjamins: 271-295.

—. 2011. *Corpus Approaches to Evaluation. Phraseology and Evaluative Language*. New York/London: Routledge.

Hyland, Ken / Tse, Polly 2004. Metadiscourse in academic writing: a reappraisal, In *Applied Linguistics* 25: 156-176.

ITTIG and Accademia della Crusca 2011. Guida alla redazione degli atti amministrativi. Regole e suggerimenti. http://www.ittig.cnr.it/Ricerca/Testi/GuidaAttiAmministrativi.pdf (accessed on 01/10/2012).

Kurzon, Dennis 2001. The politeness of judges: American and English judicial behavior. *Journal of Pragmatics* 33: 61-85.

McEnery, Tony / Xiao, Richard / Tono, Yukio 2006. *Corpus-based Language Studies. An Advanced Resource Book*. London: Routledge.

Martin, James R. / White, Peter R. 2005. *The Language of Evaluation: Appraisal in English*. London: Palgrave.

Mazzi, Davide 2007. The construction of argumentation in judicial texts: combining a genre and corpus perspective. *Argumentation* 1: 21-38.

—. 2010. This argument fails for two reasons… a linguistic analysis of judicial evaluation strategies in US Supreme Court judgements. *International Journal for the Semiotics of Law* 23(4): 373-385.

Ochs, Elinor (ed.) 1989. *The Pragmatic of Affect.* Special Issue of *Text* 9.

Palmer, Frank R. 1987. *The English Verb* 2nd Edition. London: Longman.
Philips, Susan U. 1998. *Ideology in the Language of Judges. How Judges Practice Law, Politics, and Courtroom Control*. Oxford: Oxford University Press.
Pontrandolfo, Gianluca 2013. La fraseología en las sentencias penales: un estudio contrastivo español, italiano, inglés basado en corpus. Unpublished PhD thesis, University of Trieste.
Pound, Roscoe 1910. Law in book and law in action. In *American Law Review* 44: 12-36.
Rovere, Giovanni 2000. L'avverbiale strumentale nel linguaggio giuridico. In Schena, L. / Snel Trampus, R. (eds.) *Traduttori e giuristi a confronto. Interpretazione traducente e comparazione del discorso giuridico* I. Bologna: CLUEB: 25-35.
Schulze, Rainer / Römer, Ute 2008. Patterns, meaningful units and specialized discourses. In *Intenational Journal of Corpus Linguistics* 13(3): 265-270.
Scott, Mike 2008. *WordSmith Tools version 5*, Liverpool: Lexical Analysis Software.
Sinclair, John / Coulthard, Malcolm 1975. *Towards an Analysis of Discourse: the English Used by Teachers and Pupils*. Oxford: Oxford University Press.
Solan, Lawrence M. 1993. *The Language of Judges*. Chicago: University of Chicago Press.
Taboada, Maite / Grieve, Jack 2004. Analyzing appraisal automatically. In *Proceedings of AAAI Spring Symposium on Exploring Attitude and Affect in Text. Stanford. March 2004*: 158-161.
Teubert, Wolfgang 2005. My version of corpus linguistics. *International Journal of Corpus Linguistics* 10(1): 1–13.

CHAPTER TWO

DRAFTING COURT JUDGMENTS IN ITALY: HISTORY, COMPLEXITY AND SIMPLIFICATION

STEFANO ONDELLI

Introduction

This chapter considers Italian judgments from a text-linguistic viewpoint, offering insights into their historical development and suggestions for simplification or rationalisation. The research topic was identified on the basis of the following assumptions:

- unlike other countries such as Germany, little specific training on legal drafting is provided to law students and professionals in Italy (Micali 1988);
- since no formal, institutionalised training is provided, judges and jurists develop their writing skills during their apprenticeship by imitating senior colleagues (Cortelazzo 2003);
- although general dissatisfaction with the language quality of legal documents (Mortara Garavelli 2001) has led to initiatives aimed at ensuring the effective drafting of legal texts, little attention has been paid to judicial texts (*Accademia della Crusca* 2011).

This study of Italian court judgments has been conducted in three stages. A brief summary is provided of the first two while the third is discussed in terms of the opportunities and prospects created for text-simplifying purposes.

The court judgment as a text genre

Verbs were chosen as a testing ground for the analysis of the judgment genre because of the paramount role they play at both sentence and textual levels. Moreover, the inconsistent selection of verb tenses in court judgments has often been criticised, especially when compared to texts drafted in other languages, where it is sometimes governed by explicit distribution rules (e.g. German *Formularbücher*; Vecchi 2000).

In court judgments, the present (PRE) and three past tenses of the indicative available in Italian are said to mix together inconsistently (Rega 2006) and contribute to blurring the divide between points of fact and points of law, a feature that is invariably frowned upon by legal experts (Mazzamuto 2000). But is there some discernible pattern behind this apparent confusion? And why is the imperfect tense (IPF) so commonly used in its narrative function?[1] Finally, in the light of the function and distribution (if any) of verb tenses, can we envisage drafting guidelines?

In order to answer these questions and analyse the transitions involving verb tenses along the three levels of jurisdiction of the Italian system, I put together a corpus of 63 court judgments relating to 14 cases debated in the Trieste Criminal Court of first instance, also discussed in the Trieste Court of Appeal and the Supreme Court of Cassation (*Corte Suprema di Cassazione*), and 7 cases from the Turin Criminal Court of first instance, also discussed in the Turin Court of Appeal and the Supreme Court of Cassation. A smaller corpus of 13 cases discussed in the Trieste and Turin first-instance and appeal courts was used as control data (Ondelli 2012).

It should be noted that this was a qualitative analysis: no text-mining software or other automatic techniques could be used because texts from the courts of first instance and appeal were only available in typewritten, hard copy format. The analysis of the corpus showed that the text component of the court judgment as a text genre consists in a frozen section whose function is the identification of the case at hand:

SENTENZA
IN NOME DEL POPOLO ITALIANO
IL TRIBUNALE DI […]

Composto dai Magistrati
1) (President)
2) (Judge)
3) (Judge)

[1] The IPF is normally used in Italian to express the three sub-classes of the imperfective aspect: continuous, progressive and habitual. The label *imperfetto narrativo* (narrative imperfect – NIPF) refers to the use of the imperfect in contexts which would normally require perfective tenses and is considered a very peculiar trait of Italian non-fictional prose, appearing almost exclusively in legal and institutional texts (Bertinetto 1987).

> *ha pronunziato* e *pubblicato* mediante lettura del dispositivo la seguente
> SENTENZA,
> nei confronti di [...]
> IMPUTATO
> del reato [...] perché [...] Fatto accertato in città e data.

The most apparent consequence of the interaction between the actual communicative situation, on the one hand, and the legal tradition and relevant norms (mainly article 546 of the Code of Criminal Procedure), on the other is the paradox of a text stating that it includes *itself.* As sometimes signalled explicitly in the heading, a text officially classified as a judgment claims it contains a second text, also referred to by means of the label *sentenza* ('judgment'), which was produced in the past (as signalled by the compound past – CP – *ha pronunziato e pubblicato*). In strictly legal terms, none of those texts amounts to a judgment because they both lack mandatory information.

However, immediately after the conclusions of the parties, verbs switch to the PRE or the infinitive introducing an object clause, as though the main clause with the actual request had been omitted:

> - Conclusioni del P.M.: *Chiede*, previa concessione delle attenuanti generiche prevalenti sull'aggravante contestata, la condanna alla pena di anni 5 di reclusione con tutte le conseguenze di legge. *Si oppone* all'istanza di revoca della misura cautelare ...
> - Conclusioni della difesa: in principalità *assolversi* perché il fatto non sussiste o per non aver commesso il fatto.

The examples above show that a court judgment is the result of a cut-and-paste process from other texts, which in turn produces confusing consequences for verb tense patterns.

According to Article 546 of the Italian Code of Criminal Procedure, judgments must provide the grounds for the decision, along with a brief summary of the relevant facts. However, the survey of the corpus showed that, even in judgments produced by courts of first instance, the next text section is an account of the legal procedures that the case has undergone before being heard in court.

> - Avverso la predetta sentenza *proponeva* appello il difensore dell'imputato con atto depositato il 3.5.95, con il quale *criticava* la decisione del Tribunale...
> - All'udienza del 21.3.1995 [...] *venivano* esaminati i testi del P.M. ed acquisita la documentazione prodotta dalle parti.
> - L'accezione *è* infondata e *va* respinta

The IPF is used to describe a sequence of events which in Italian is normally expressed by the CP or simple past (SP) tenses, until the sequence is closed by a sentence in the PRE passing a judgment on the matter and anticipating the final decision. The NIPF is constantly used in the text section under scrutiny; then the actual grounds for the decision begin, at which point the PRE is used to describe the provisions of the laws being enforced and all three past tenses – including the IPF – are again used according to the traditional distribution envisaged by Italian grammar:

> - Questi fatti *consentono* con evidenza di affermare la penale responsabilità del …
> - La norma citata *impone* l'obbligo del segreto …
> - *È* infatti *emerso* che l'odierno imputato, con fare rapidissimo, *sollevò* da terra con il braccio sinistro il bimbo …
> - ... lo *estrassero* a forza dall'automobile, ed egli si *oppose* [...] e *pronunciò* altresì la frase minacciosa ...

The actual decision – the so-called operative part of the judgment – again envisages an inconsistent tense shift. While the PRE commenting upon the legal provisions for implementation may be considered a-temporal (i.e. a law envisages a provision now, did so in the past and will do so in the future), the PRE used in the operative part is clearly performative and deictic: the court does something in legal terms when it states its decision (acquittal, discharge and so on). Like the conclusions of the parties, the operative part is clearly the result of a cut-and-paste procedure affecting tense distribution in the text:

> La doglianza dell'appellante *è*, poi, inconferente ...
> *Va* quindi dichiarata la penale responsabilità degli imputati in ordine a tutti i reati ascritti.
>
> P.Q.M.
>
> Il Tribunale, visti gli artt. 483, 487, 488 c.p.p./30
>
> *DICHIARA*
>
> […] colpevole del reato ascritto ...

The table below accounts for the correlation among structural elements composing the text, the pragmatic function and sub-functions fulfilled by each section, and the tendential tense distribution (Ondelli 2011a). "Tendential" is an important caveat because the NIPF tends to encroach on the grounds for the decision, so that all past events are expressed by the IPF – be it proper or narrative.

Structural element	Pragmatic function & sub-components	Tense
Introduction	Normative	CP
Account of proceedings	Narrative	NIPF
Grounds for the decision	ARGUMENTATIVE - Narrative, descriptive, prescriptive	PRE - CP PS PRE
Decision	Normative	PRE

Table 2-1 – Generic structure and verb tense distribution in Italian court judgments

The alternation between present and past perspectives may be explained in terms of the actual production of the text[2] and of a cut-and-paste drafting procedure, but explaining the presence of the NIPF is more difficult (Ondelli 2008). Arguably, it is a stylistic marker providing a more solemn and institutional tone to the texts produced by judges. The Supreme Court of Cassation – given its prestige – could be responsible for the insurgence of this stylistic trait, imitated by the lower courts.

The preliminary conclusions after the first stage of the research are the following:

- the generic structure potential (Halliday / Hasan 1989) of Italian judgments is the outcome of historical evolution rather than of the immediate contextual configuration;
- the selection of stylistic traits and the arrangement of contents are not always justified from a functional viewpoint;
- the impact of the actual contextual configuration is clearly discernible in the inconsistent use of verb tenses.

A historical survey

To confirm the preliminary conclusions, stage two of the research project examined the historical development of Italian court judgments. Again, no automatic text mining tools could be used because no collections of older texts are available in electronic format. A corpus was extracted from the review *Il Foro Italiano*, which publishes – among other things – influential judgments mainly originated by the Supreme Court of Cassation (Ondelli 2011b).

The analysis focused on criminal court judgments published after 1876 (the first issue appeared shortly after the unification of the judicial systems

[2] This is because the operative part is read aloud in court, while the grounds for the decision are usually written at a later stage.

in Italy, following political unification in 1861). One volume per decade was analysed (1947 replaced 1946, when very few texts were published after the Second World War). Additional surveys were conducted on the occasion of significant changes, such as the establishment of a single Criminal Court of Cassation in Rome in 1888; the introduction of a national Code of Criminal Procedure for the Kingdom of Italy in 1913 and subsequent reforms (Codice Rocco in 1930 and Codice Vassalli in 1988). As far as statutory provisions are concerned, the articles regulating court judgments[3] do not differ significantly in the four codes since they basically require the same items, virtually in the same order.

In the 1876 volume, judgments are constantly characterised by the *phrase unique* inherited from the French *Cour de Cassation* (Gorla 1967) and the whole text is structured like a syllogism. At this stage the NIPF is absent and the SP dominates the points of fact. In the following decade (1876-1886), although total occurrences still form a very small minority, the NIPF emerges as what in French is labelled the *imparfait d'ouverture et de clôture* (Caruso 1997: 118-120), i.e. at the beginning and/or end of narrations, a trait that is quite common in literary texts (Bertinetto 1986). In the period from 1886 to 1926, the SP still dominates the grounds for the decision and the NIPF starts to appear. However, it is only used for declarative verbs, mainly the opening and closing sections of the points of fact.

Although the transition gains momentum from the late 1930s, the key turning point takes place in the aftermath of the Second World War. When the *phrase unique* is abandoned, the NIPF/SP alternate and the NIPF becomes more frequent in judgments of the first-instance and appeal Courts, which in turn are published more frequently than in previous volumes. After the 1970s, the current tendential tense distribution illustrated under §2 becomes the norm.

After the second stage of the research, yet more (invariably) preliminary conclusions can be advanced. The analysis of judgments published in *Il Foro Italiano* over the last 150 years shows that the SP was originally used to report past events, followed by the gradual emergence and partial specialisation of the NIPF. Again, no causes or functional justifications for this new distinctive trait are apparent: some jurists and historians claim that, after the 1960s, judges lost their prestige and gradually turned into bureaucrats (Guarnieri 1995). If that is the case, we might see the NIPF as a linguistic stereotype deriving from this change of status.

[3] In terms of content, nothing is envisaged in matters of form and certainly not the use of verb tenses.

Looking for alternatives

According to the historical survey described above, the emergence of the NIPF was a bottom-up rather than a top-down process, i.e. instead of "descending" from prestigious models, such as the Supreme Court of Cassation, the NIPF may have "risen" from preparatory judicial texts, such as police reports and the like. Nonetheless, it still holds true that the use and expansion of the NIPF is one of the factors contributing to the widely criticised obscurity of the language of Italian judges. In order to look for alternative models pointing to simplification, stage three of the research consisted in a preliminary survey of judgments written in Italian where subjects operated beyond national boundaries.

We compiled a new corpus which, for obvious reasons (i.e. the competences of the CJEU), was not limited to criminal cases. Rather, it encompassed a wide range of subject matters in order to counterbalance the impact of contents on the language. The CJEU sub-corpus provided the selection criteria for three other sub-corpora in terms of both the time span (texts produced after the 2009 Lisbon Treaty) and the variety of subject matter considered. The overall corpus was composed as follows:

- 132 judgments of the Italian Supreme Court of Civil Cassation (CASS), taken from the *De Jure* data bank[4]: texts were produced by all chambers including joint sittings; average text length: 2,110.10; min-max range: 286-9,442 tokens;
- 59 judgments of the CJEU;[5] texts produced by all chambers including the grand chamber; all texts were references for preliminary rulings whose source was Italy and, consequently, the authentic language of the cases was Italian; average text length: 4,683.88; min-max range: 2,244-8,425 tokens.
- 133 judgments of the Swiss Federal Court (FED);[6] texts produced by all chambers except the criminal chamber; average text length: 2,080.45; min-max range: 140-12,804 tokens;
- 111 judgments of the Ticino Cantonal Court of Appeal (TIC);[7] texts produced by all chambers except the criminal chamber; average text length: 2,502.95; min-max range: 507-15,242.

---

[4] http://dejure.giuffre.it

[5] The texts were retrieved from the website http://curia.europa.eu.

[6] The texts were retrieved from the website http://www.bger.ch.

[7] The texts were retrieved from the website http://www4.ti.ch.

Since the corpus was available in electronic format, it was assessed using statistical text analysis tools in order to ascertain whether differences in terms of complexity emerged from a quantitative perspective. Preliminary "cleansing" involved the removal of all numbers. This was done because they were liable to impact greatly on lexicometric measures, especially in the case of the judgments of the CJEU, in which all paragraphs are numbered and references are very frequently made to legal documents identified by means of dates and numbers.

Moreover, the initial "frozen" case-identifying sections along with the court and the parties were removed from all texts, so that the corpus includes all components loosely contributing to the grounds for the decision and the operative part. This was done in order to prevent the most fixed and repetitive sections from affecting measures such as lexical richness. In addition, the analysis focused on text components allowing a relatively greater freedom of expression in order to obtain a reliable account of the Italian used by the judges of the four courts. This strategy also accounts for the extreme brevity of some of the texts included in the corpus. As shown by the number of texts per sub-corpus, the judgments of the CJEU are longer than all the others, which in turn prove relatively similar in terms of average length.

The starting assumption of the analysis was that the complexity and obscurity of the language used by Italian judges should emerge in comparison with their European and – possibly – Swiss counterparts. The lexical measures of the sub-corpora were calculated by means of *Taltac2*, a statistical analysis tool developed by the University of Rome "La Sapienza" (http://www.taltac.it):

	CASS	**CJEU**	**FED**	**TIC**
N	276,424	276,349	276,700	277,827
V	14,202	10,986	13,360	16,272
(V/N)*100	5.138	3.975	4.828	5.857
(V1/V)*100	38.072	35.654	39.873	40.118
N/V	19.464	25.155	20.711	17.074
V/sqrN	27.012	20.898	25.398	30.871
a	1.310	1.347	1.319	1.293

Table 2-2 Lexical measures

Table 2-2 shows that the four sub-corpora are virtually identical in size (N, i.e. number of tokens) and may be considered lexically rich, as shown by V/sqrN and the *a* index (Tuzzi 2003: 127). The lexical richness ((V/N)*100 – where V is the number of types) – and number of hapax legomena ((V1/V)*100) of the texts produced by the CJEU are markedly smaller than the others. Content variety may account for the TIC producing texts that are lexically richer than those of the FED and CASS, but this is an unlikely explanation for the very significant gap in the case of the CJEU, since references for preliminary rulings in CJEU deal with a broad range of matters. Rather, the explanatory factors here might include the greater consistency required from European judges in order to ensure the constant use of shared terminology (Capotorti 1988: 243-244; Preite 2008) and – possibly – the universals of translation, namely simplification and normalisation (Baker 1996): although the authentic language for all the texts included in the corpus is Italian, they are certainly all translations, almost exclusively from French (Gallo 2005).

From the lexical viewpoint, the texts produced in the European Union seem to be less complex than those drafted by national judges. Unfortunately, this conclusion is not supported by the incidence of basic vocabulary (i.e. the approximately 7000 most frequent words in Italian measured by means of the software provided in De Mauro 1997).

	CASS	CJEU	FED	TIC
Fundamental	65.21	61.07	63.96	64.16
High use	8.65	11.91	10.17	9.64
Highly available	7.57	7.61	8.11	8.31
Non-BV	18.58	19.41	17.76	17.89
Tokens analysed	16,365	16,368	16,356	16,363

Table 2-3 Basic Vocabulary distribution (%)

Although the data reported in Table 2-3 only refer to samples of just above 16,000 tokens (i.e. the upper limit of the software processing capacity), the trend illustrated in the Table above is reversed: if the non-BV share is accepted as an indicator of lexical complexity, then the judgments of the CJEU may be considered lexically more difficult than those produced by the three national courts. Moreover, within the BV, the share of fundamental words is also smaller for the CJEU texts, and this may indicate that EU-level judges resort to more "technical" terminology, which is less likely to be found in everyday language (Goffin 1997:71; Cosmai 2000: 11). However, they then may use it more consistently and repeatedly, also helped by supervision of the *lecteurs d'arrêts* (McAuliffe 2010). By contrast, national judges may tend to avoid repetitions and use BV synonyms or paraphrases, thus leading to the marked lexical variation typical of any piece of Italian prose.

Lexical density (Halliday 1989: 61; De Mauro et al. 1993: 123), generally regarded as a factor contributing to the complexity of texts, may be calculated after POS-tagging the corpus by means of *Treetagger*, a probabilistic software tool developed by Helmut Schmid at the University of Stuttgart.[8] Since errors are statistically distributed, data relating to the sub-corpora may be considered comparable: the higher the ratio of content words (nouns, adverbs and verbs) to grammatical words (pronouns, prepositions, conjunctions, adverbs, determiners and interjections), the more complex a text. Percentages do not add up to 100 because Table 2-4 below does not account for symbols, abbreviations and other infrequent labels attributed by *Treetagger*, which are not relevant for a classification aimed at calculating lexical density.

	CASS	CJEU	FED	TIC
Content Words				
nouns %	91,586 33.13	93,063 33.68	92,523 33.44	92,826 33.41
adjectives %%	27,581 9.98	29,480 10.67	27,424 9.91	24,873 8.95
verbs %	39,357 14.24	37,491 13.57	43,145 15.59	40,478 14.57
adverbs %	12,194 4.41	8,986 3.25	13,403 4.84	12,518 4.51
total CW %	**170,718 61.76**	**169,020 61.16**	**176,495 63.79**	**170,695 61.44**
Grammatical words				
determiners %	19,161 6.93	18,835 6.82	20,775 7.51	19,390 6.98
conjunctions %	10,539 3.81	11,075 4.08	10,019 3.62	9,743 3.51
interjections %	111 0.04	87 0.03	56 0.02	52 0.02
prepositions %	56,061 2.02	57,601 2.08	49,599 1.79	48,331 1.74
pronouns %	13,242 4.79	14,946 5.41	12,321 4.45	13,484 4.85
total GW %	**99,114 35.86**	**102,544 37.11**	**92,770 33.53**	**91.000 32.75**

Table 2-4 Lexical density

Except for minor erratic variations, such as the unusually low percentage of adverbs in the CJEU sub-corpus or the high share of verbs in the FED corpus etc., POS distribution is virtually equivalent in all the sub-corpora, with a slightly higher share of content words in the texts of the

[8] http://www.ims.uni-stuttgart.de/projekte/corplex/TreeTagger.

FED. The only conclusion that may be drawn here is that the overwhelming majority of content words clearly shows that judgments belong to the category of (perhaps semantically very dense) Italian written texts (Cresti 2005).

Another indicator of complexity is the *Gulpease* index, specifically developed by the University of Rome "La Sapienza" to measure the readability of Italian texts. The four sub-corpora were processed by means of the *Autogulp* software (Piemontese 1996).

	CASS	**CJEU**	**FED**	**TIC**
Gulpease index	40.89	40.08	40.96	48.70
Word length				
1-3 letters	39.60	36.97	40.84	42.36
4-10 letters	50.90	53.89	51.26	49.95
> 10 letters	9.50	9.14	7.90	7.69
Average length	5.40	5.52	5.35	5.23
Sentence length				
1-7 words	25.89	16.87	30.21	26.73
8-20 words	12.20	13.44	9.18	24.30
> 20	61.91	69.70	60.61	48.97
Average length	51.14	47.89	54.89	24.90

Table 2-5 Readability values

In terms of this readability score, the TIC sub-corpus stands out, whereas the other three courts obtain values approaching 40. It seems clear that, regardless of the different distribution of the number of letters, the discriminating factor is not word length but sentence length, with the sentences of the TIC sub-corpus being on average half as long as those of the other sub-corpora. Unfortunately, this indicator is not very reliable in texts such as court judgments, which are strongly characterised by internal titles, subheadings, bullet point lists and isolated expressions interrupted by the end-of-line command and are also liable to be counted by the software as full sentences, thus affecting average length values. This is also confirmed by the completely inconsistent results obtained after POS-tagging the corpus using *Treetagger*, which marks as SENT all punctuation marks signalling the end of sentences. The average sentence length values obtained by dividing the number of tokens by the number of end-of-sentence punctuation marks are completely inconsistent with the *Gulpease* results in two (CASS and FED) out of four sub-corpora.

	CASS	CJEU	FED	TIC
SENT	8,209	6,107	15,516	12,448
av. sentence l.	33.67	45.25	17.83	22.32

Table 2-6 Average sentence length (based on *Treetagger*)

However, for the purposes of this study, it is probably tense distribution after POS-tagging which provides the most interesting information (negligible amounts of imperative and reflexive infinitive forms are not reported).

	CASS	CJEU	FED	TIC
Present	8.539 3.09	11,150 4.03	13,217 4.78	11,735 4.22
Future	65 0.02	99 0.04	239 0.09	251 0,09
Imperfect	2,983 1.08	538 0.19	1,279 0.46	1,402 0.50
Simple Past	217 0.08	23 0.01	93 0.03	104 0.04
Perfect Participle	15,199 5.50	11,211 4.06	15,212 5.50	13,943 5.02
Present Participle	755 0.27	790 0.29	734 0.26	568 0.20
Gerund	1,950 0.71	1,178 0.43	1,354 0.49	1,668 0.60
Infinitive	5,342 1.93	6,594 2.38	6,664 2.41	6,686 2.41
Conditional	738 0.27	629 0.23	1,011 0.36	856 0.31
Present Subjunctive	1,196 0.43	2,224 0.80	1,151 0.42	1,039 0.37
Imperfect Subjunctive	471 0.17	179 0.06	396 0.14	505 0.18
Total Subjunctive	1,667 0.60	2,403 0.87	1,547 0.56	1,544 0.56

Table 2-7 Verb tense distribution (tokens and %)

As shown in Table 2-7, the density of the IPF tense[9] is strikingly more frequent in the CASS, as are to a lesser extent the SP and gerund: the former, virtually absent in the judgments of the CJEU, may be regarded as a

[9] Of course *Treetagger* cannot distinguish between the narrative and other uses.

trait contributing to a conservative use of the Italian language[10], while the latter is often frowned upon by plain language advocates since it leads to excessive information density and makes the identification of the sentence subject troublesome (Cortelazzo / Pellegrino 2003).

Since *Treetagger* is unable to identify the CP and counts auxiliary verbs and past participles as independent entries, both data are particularly meaningful. Given that the NIPF replaces both perfective pasts, as may be expected, the PRE share drops in the CASS sub-corpus, but this is not the case with the past participle. In other words, Italian judges, when describing past events, not only make abundant use of the IPF and SP, but also of participial clauses – another trait contributing to the information density and syntactic complexity of Italian judgments (Cortelazzo / Pellegrino 2003). Since European and Swiss judges use the IPF and SP less frequently than their Italian counterparts, the higher shares of PRE and past participle forms may be explained by their more frequent use of the CP, which in turn may be attributed to the influence of the original French text in the CJEU and to the Northern variety of Italian spoken and written in Switzerland.

If the quantitative analysis conducted by means of automatic tools is abandoned in favour of qualitative, manual surveys, then a closer look at tense distribution within all textual sections will show that the models implemented in Switzerland avoid the paradox of a text containing itself by omitting the CP form after the identification of the court. And, although the four types of judgments under scrutiny belong to the same continental legal tradition, the models will consequently also solve the inconsistency of an operative part in the PRE tense after an introductory section in the CP tense.

In Swiss judgments, the NIPF is extremely rare. A peculiarity that emerges, but still needs to be analysed in detail, is the frequent use of the conditional mood to signal reported speech, as emerges from the frequency values reported in Table 2-7. The CJEU produces texts that, despite lexicometric differences, are similar to their Italian counterparts in terms of the reference to the judgment contained within the judgment, introduced by a declarative verb in the CP. Moreover, within the richly articulated text segment identifiable as the grounds for the decision, the NIPF emerges quite frequently in the account of the previous proceedings. This sometimes leads to an erratic mix of verb tenses (CP, IPF and PRE, but the SP is almost absent) resembling Italian patterns. Brief surveys on other

[10] The CP is an innovative trait which is gaining ground in everyday language (Bertinetto 1986).

types of judgments produced by the CJEU revealed no apparent correlation with subject matter, language of origin or procedure.

CJEU	FED	TIC
Heading "Sentenza della Corte" + identification of the parties and case.	**Identification of the Court** (no deictic reference to the following sub-text).	**Identification of the Court** (no deictic reference to the following sub-text).
Identification of the Court + deictic reference to the following sub-text (CP: *ha pronunciato la seguente sentenza*)	Identification of the parties and case. No verb.	Identification of the parties and case. No verb.
Several subsection headings (legal background, points of facts, previous proceedings etc.). Paragraphs identified by letters and numbers. NIPF emerges frequently in the account of the previous proceedings, sometimes leading to an erratic mix of verb tenses (CP, PRE but SP is absent) resembling the Italian patterns.	**Facts** (signalled by heading). Paragraphs identified by letters and numbers. CP (SP is very rare).	**Facts** (signalled by heading). Paragraphs identified by letters and numbers. CP (SP is very rare).
	Law (signalled by heading). CP/PRE.	**Law** (signalled by heading). CP/PRE.
Operative part (*Per questi motivi).* PRE with declarative verbs (*dichiara e statuisce*) + object clauses	**Operative part** (*Per questi motivi*). PRE with declarative verbs (*Il Presidente/il Tribunale pronuncia*) + object clauses	**Operative part** (*Per questi motivi/per i quali motivi/*). PRE with declarative verbs (*pronuncia* or *dichiara e* pronuncia; rarely: *decide/ decreta*) + object clauses

Table 2-8 Generic structure and verb tense distribution in judgments produced by the CJEU, FED and TIC

Once again, preliminary conclusions regarding stage three of the current research project may be summarised as follows:

- automatic text-mining tools undeniably show some limitations. Nonetheless, they may prove helpful in analysing other complexity factors in Italian judgments – other than verb tenses – which have been criticised in the literature (Mortara Garavelli 2001), such as adjectives and past participles positioned before nouns, other peculiar word orders, the selection of archaic and high-register vocabulary especially in the case of connecting words, subjects in the post-verbal position, etc.;

- conversely, data obtained through automatic analyses may draw the researcher's attention to distinctive traits of judgments drafted by different courts, as is the case with the reported speech conditional in the Swiss sub-corpora or the unusual frequency of the subjunctive mood in European judgments (Table 2-7);
- in particular, statistical surveys may provide evidence of the peculiarities of the drafting procedure of judgments produced by the CJEU (namely the translation process and the marked terminological consistency and intertextuality);
- as shown by the qualitative analysis of verb tense distribution within text components, foreign models may be used as examples for simplification purposes. Swiss judgments have already proven interesting in terms of the absence of the NIPF and a more consistent use of verb tenses. Future investigations may be broadened to include texts drafted in the bilingual Court of Rovinj, Croatia.

References

Accademia della Crusca 2011. *Guida alla redazione degli atti amministrativi. Regole e suggerimenti*, a cura del gruppo di lavoro promosso da Istituto di teoria e tecniche dell'informazione giuridica e Accademia della Crusca, 2011. Available from:
http://www.ittig.cnr.it/Ricerca/Testi/GuidaAttiAmministrativi.pdf.

Baker, Mona 1996. Corpus-based Translation Studies: the Challenges that Lie Ahead. In Somers, H. L. (ed.) *Terminology,LSP and Translation. Studies in Language Engineering in Honour of Juan C. Sager.* Amsterdam: John Benjamins: 175-186.

Bertinetto, Pier Marco 1986. *Tempo, aspetto e azione nel verbo italiano. Il sistema dell'indicativo*. Firenze: Accademia della Crusca.

—. 1987. Structure and origin of the "narrative" imperfect. In Giacalone Ramat, A. / Carruba, O. / Bernini, G. (eds.) *Papers from the 7th International Conference on Historical Linguistics..* Amsterdam/Philadelphia: John Benjamins: 71-85.

Capotorti, Francesco 1988. La sentenza della Corte di Giustiza delle Comunità Europee". In AA.VV. *La sentenza in Europa. Metodo, tecnica e stile*. Padova: CEDAM: 230-247.

Caruso, Vincenzo 1997. *Lo stile delle sentenze. Analisi comparata di testi giurisprudenziali italiani, francesi e inglesi.* Trieste: Università degli Studi di Trieste (unpublished dissertation).

Cortelazzo, Michele A. 2003. La tacita codificazione della testualità delle sentenze. In Mariani Marini, A. (ed.) *La lingua, la legge, la professione forense*. Milano: Giuffrè: 79-88.

Cortelazzo, Michele A. / Pellegrino, Federica 2003. *Guida alla scrittura istituzionale*. Roma-Bari: Laterza.

Cosmai, Domenico 2000. La lingua dell'Unione europea. Problemi redazionali e traduttivi. *Jornal da Associaçao Portuguesa de Traductores* 25: 11-17.

Cresti, Emanuela 2005. Brevi note sulle principali strategie lessicali e strutturali del parlato di quattro lingue romanze (italiano, francese, portoghese e spagnolo): dati dal corpus C-ORAL-ROM. In Korzen, I. (ed.) *Lingua cultura e intercultura: l'italiano e le altre lingue*, *Atti del VIII Convegno SILFI (Copenaghen, 22-26 giugno 2004) Frederiksberg*. Copenhagen: Samfundslitteratur Press. Available from: http://lablita.dit.unifi.it/preprint/preprint-CRESTI-SILFI-04.pdf: 163-176.

De Mauro, Tullio / Mancini, Federico / Vedovelli, Massimo / Voghera, Miriam (eds.) 1993. *Lessico di Frequenza dell'italiano parlato*. Milano: Etas libri.

De Mauro, Tullio 1997, *Guida all'uso delle parole*. Roma: Editori riuniti.

Gallo, Giovanni 2005. La lingua italiana nei testi della Corte di giustizia delle Comunità europee. In *Atti della Prima giornata della Rete di eccellenza dell'italiano istituzionale*. Bruxelles: Commissione europea. Available from: http://ec.europa.eu/dgs/translation/rei/documenti/giornate/irei_gallo.pdf.

Goffin, Roger 1997. L'Eurolecte: le langage d'une Europe communautaire en devenir. *Terminologie et Traduction* 1: 63-73.

Gorla, Gino 1967. Lo stile delle sentenze. Ricerca storico-comparativa. *Quaderni de «Il Foro italiano»*, 314-362.

Guarnieri, Carlo 1995. L'ordine pubblico e la giustizia penale. In Romanelli, R. (ed.) *Storia dello Stato italiano dall'Unità a oggi*. Roma: Donzelli: 365-405.

Halliday, Michael A.K. 1989. *Spoken and Written Language*. Oxford: Oxford University Press.

Halliday, Michael A.K. / Hasan, Ruqaiya 1989. *Language, Context and Text. Aspects of Language in a Social-Semiotic Perspective*. Oxford: Oxford University Press.

Mazzamuto, Salvatore 2000, Relazione introduttiva. In Vacca, L. (ed.) *Lo stile delle sentenze e l'utilizzazione dei precedenti: profili storico-comparatistici*. Torino: Giappichelli: 7-20.

McAuliffe, Karen 2010. Translating the Law: the need for hybridity in EU law. In *Colloque international Traduire la diversité* (Liège, 6-8 mai 2010). Available from: http://www.l3.ulg.ac.be/colloquetraduction2010/textes.html.

Micali, Giovanni 1988. Lo stile delle sentenze della Corte di Cassazione. *Giustizia Civile*, II: 26-38.

Mortara Garavelli, Bice 2001. *Le parole e la giustizia. Divagazioni grammaticali e retoriche su testi giuridici italiani*. Torino: Einaudi.

Ondelli, Stefano 2008. The 'narrative imperfect' in legal Italian: the case of judgements. *Fachsprache* 1-2: 43-55.

—. 2011a. Verb tense distribution and pragmatic functions in Italian Court Judgments. *Revista de Llengua i Dret* 55: 13-34.

—. 2011b. Evoluzione di un genere testuale: la sentenza penale nell'Italia postunitaria. In Nesi, A. / Morgana, S. / Maraschio, N. (eds.) *Storia della lingua italiana e storia dell'Italia unita. L'italiano e lo stato nazionale, Atti del IX Convegno ASLI (Associazione per la Storia della Lingua Italiana), (Firenze, 2-4 dicembre 2010)*. Firenze: Franco Cesati Editore: 451-462.

—. 2012. *La sentenza penale tra azione e narrazione. Un'analisi pragmalinguistica*. Padova: CLEUP.

Piemontese, Maria Emanuela 1996. *Capire e farsi capire. Teorie e tecniche della scrittura controllata*. Napoli: Tecnodid.

Preite, Chiara 2008. La sentenza della corte di giustizia delle comunità europee: eterogeneità sequenziale ed enunciativa. In Garzone, G. / Santulli, F. (eds.) *Il linguaggio giuridico: prospettive interdisciplinari*. Milano: Giuffrè: 261-283.

Rega, Lorenza 2006. Riflessioni sulla traduzione giuridica tedesco-italiano-tedesco. In Benelli, G. / Tonini, G. (eds.) *Studi in ricordo di Carmen Sanchez Montero* 2.. Trieste: DSLIT, Università degli studi di Trieste, 401-420.

Tuzzi, Arjuna 2003. *L'analisi del contenuto. Introduzione ai metodi e alle tecniche di ricerca*. Roma: Carocci.

Vecchi, Paolo M. 2000. Il modello tedesco In Vacca, L. (ed.) *Lo stile delle sentenze e l'utilizzazione dei precedenti: profili storico-comparatistici*. Torino: Giappichelli: 139-155.

CHAPTER THREE

SELF-CONSTRUCTION OF LEGISLATIVE DISCOURSE THROUGH MASHUPS: A MULTI-PERSPECTIVE ANALYSIS

ANNA FRANCA PLASTINA

Introduction

The average layperson's comprehension of legal documents is often challenged by the obscure, ambiguous and complex nature of legal discourse. Unlike most other professional discourses, all legislative texts are, in the first place, addressed to ordinary people, who should be able to interpret them semantically and pragmatically (cf. Gambaro 2007). Their high density of information and excessive length (cf. Bhatia 1987; Bhatia and Bhatia 2011) can, however, easily burden the ordinary reader. The demand for all-inclusiveness may make the cognitive structuring of these texts unclear to the reader who lacks professional and generic knowledge of their organisation (cf. Bhatia 1993). Problems may also arise due to the structural complexity of the language employed, which appears as "[…] linguistic nonsense that is pompous, verbose, flabby and circumlocutory" (Slapper / Kelly 2001: 8). Charnock (2006) underlines how this is unfortunate as ordinary readers may be unaware of their rights and obligations, despite the fact that *ignorantia legis neminem excusat* (ignorance of the law excuses no one).

As the easiest solution, the uninitiated reader may attempt to simplify legislative texts to make sense of them. However, this "[…] may obscure or even destroy the integrity of the text in question […]" (Bhatia 1993: 196). On the other hand, *easification devices* offer a more pragmatic solution to "guide the reader through the text without making any drastic changes to the content or linguistic form […]" (Bhatia 1993: 146).

In line with the non-linear rhetorical devices (charts, diagrams, figures, pictures etc.) suggested by Bhatia (2004) as possible easification devices, new multimedia technologies may be explored towards this end. Their potential is at the heart of ongoing debates within the specialist community as they are nowadays permeating law practice (cf. Feigenson et al. 2005). While "modern law is very language-oriented and is sceptical, even dismissive of images" (Boehme-Nessler 2010: 90), there is a "[…] felt need for a new visual rhetoric suitable to the digital visual age […]" (Sherwin 2011: 190) of law practice.

The potential of multimedia technologies, however, has yet to be fully explored in supporting the non-specialist community, whose problem of comprehending legislative discourse still remains largely unsolved. Laypeople are faced with unusual demands imposed on their *general law-text knowledge* and *specific knowledge* of a particular law (cf. Gunnarsson 2009) by legal discourse, which "[…] display[s] a variety and depth of intertextual and interdiscursive links rarely noticed in any other discourse" (Bhatia 1998).

In this regard, Bazerman (2004) suggests considering *intrasystem intertextuality* which, as Blackledge (2005) argues, senses previous discourses on the same subject and works at their recontextualisation. In a synchronic perspective, Fiske (1987) advocates the importance of *vertical intertextuality*, which operates across several media and social contexts. In this variety of intertextuality, relations are established between *primary* texts as vehicles of central meaning, *secondary* texts as their reviews, and *tertiary* texts, which are contributed by media consumers. Tertiary texts "may be understood as a […] means of making explicit, retrievable, modifiable, and communicable what might have remained a more or less random association" (Jensen 2003: 279) in primary texts.

In the digital context, intertextuality operates between text files as *hypertextuality* and between multimodal files as *hypermediality* so that new discourses can be consumed. However, "the intertextual transformation (recontextualization) of social meanings and values can only be adequately theorized in terms of a *social semiotics of action*" (Thibault 1991: 136-137). Intertextuality is therefore an integral aspect of the concept of context together with socio-cultural knowledge (cf. Fairclough et al. 2011).

On the other hand, interdiscursivity needs to be considered in terms of social practices and structures (cf. van Dijk 2004). Fairclough (2003: 218), for instance, points out that interdiscursive analysis "[…] mediates between linguistic analysis of a text and various forms of social analysis of social events and practices". In a social semiotic perspective, Scollon and Scollon (2003: 193) introduce the concept of *interdiscursive dialogicality* and argue that:

> […] several discourses co-exist simultaneously in a particular semiotic aggregate but none of the discourses is really internally altered by the presence of the other discourse. They operate quite independently semiotically; nevertheless, their co-presence produces a kind of dialogicality between them so that each takes part of its meaning from the co-presence of the other.

This view is further advocated by Bhatia (2008: 162), who argues for "a more comprehensive and serious look at 'interdiscursivity', which can be viewed as appropriation of semiotic resources across genres, professional practices and disciplinary cultures". This is also the stance taken in this chapter, which focuses on the practice of self-constructing discourse for the purpose of making sense of US bills, or the legislative proposals made before Congress. Social-constructivist studies have focused on acculturation into the discursive practices in the workplace (cf. Beaufort 2000) "through which novices become socialized into professional practices, a process of 'social apprenticeship' " (Orna-Montesinos 2012: 11). This study assumes that by constructing their own discourses of US bills, ordinary citizens may gain acculturation into these discursive practices. It further suggests that web-based applications, such as mashups, can be a feasible multimodal alternative (cf. Kress / van Leeuwen 2001) toward this end.

Mashups allow the juxtaposition of multimodal information from two or more different sources (Lamb 2007), and its customisation according to user needs (cf. Yu et al. 2008; Plastina 2012). In this respect, mashups are considered in the study as possible non-linear rhetorical easification devices which support the layperson's understanding of bills. For this purpose, it is necessary to generate related mashups and analyse their semiotic discourses in a multi-dimensional frame. While this practice may raise some concerns, the study assumes that the generic integrity of bills "is not static, fixed or prescribed, but is often flexible, negotiable […]" (Bhatia 2004: 123).

In this view, the analysis is framed within the multi-perspective model (Bhatia 2004), in which discourse is seen to function in three interrelated spaces: *social, professional* and *tactical*, and *textual*. Starting from text-external factors of bills, which operate in the broader *social space* of discourse, the analysis identifies the semiotic resources employed in mashed-up texts to gain social and pragmatic knowledge for full interpretation of discourse (cf. Bhatia 2008). Features are then analysed in the overlapping *professional and tactical space*, where discourse is shaped by professional practice and knowledge, and by those conventional generic resources tactically exploited by bill sponsors for the rhetorical purpose of obtaining approval. The resulting text-external factors are then related to the overlapping *textual space*, where text-internal features are examined in terms of gaining knowledge about the language structure of bills.

Although there are a number of variables which contribute to making bills incomprehensible, this study focuses on three of the most important: information load, cognitive structuring, and syntactic and lexical complexity. As these may create problems at different levels, the analysis covers all three multi-perspective spaces for processes of easification.

Materials and Method

Bills are the most customary form of legislative proposals used by both the House of Representatives (H.R.) and the Senate (S) of the US Congress (H. Con. Res. 190, 2007, Part IV). Bills originating in the House of Representatives, however, better reflect the wishes of the majority of American citizens in the lawmaking process of important social issues. Three H.R. bills pertaining to matters that affect the general public or classes of citizens, such as Water Resources Development (H.R. 1495, 110th Congress, 1st session), Quality Healthcare (H.R. 3200, 111th Congress, 1st session) and Child Gun Safety (H.R. 227, 112th Congress, 1st session) form the corpus of the materials used as *primary* texts in the study.

A specialised mashup, namely, *where a Bill becomes a Law* (www.whereabill.org), was used for the analysis. The three bills used as the corpus of materials were mashed up, and the resulting tertiary texts were subjected to qualitative, descriptive and multi-perspective analysis. The aim of the analysis was to shed light on how easification occurred in the generated texts in terms of reduction of information load, clarification of cognitive structuring, and minimisation of language complexity (cf. Bhatia 1983, 1987, 1993).

Within the aim of creating a deeper interaction between general readers or citizens and legislative texts and a link between complex language and other semiotic systems, the present analysis is informed by the cultural practice of mashups:

> The purpose of a typical Web 2.0 mashup is not to allegorise particular applications, but rather, by selectively sampling in dynamic fashion, to subvert applications to perform something they could not do otherwise by themselves (Navas 2010: 169).

Findings and Discussion

Findings are presented and discussed with reference to the multi-perspective frame of the three discourse spaces.

Easification in the *Social Space* of Bills

Deictics are employed to make discourse accessible to the reader (cf. Levinson 2004) and to facilitate the direct observation of the physical world (cf. Marmaridou 2000). Spatial, temporal and social deictics draw on readers' social and pragmatic knowledge for correct spatial and temporal localisation, as well as for understanding the social role played by the persons involved. Inexpert readers, who lack this knowledge, are not fully supported in setting the physical context of discourse by the introductory part of bills as in example (1):

(1)
In the House of Representatives
March 13, 2007
Mr. Oberstar (for himself and Ms. Eddie Bernice Johnson of Texas) introduced the following bill; which was referred to the Committee on Transportation and Infrastructure (H.R. 1495).

In this example, the spatial deictic *in* delimits the general spatial context of the Bill, while the deictic particle *the* denotes the specificity of the place, identified with *House of Representatives*. Here, the reader may lack social knowledge about this venue and its institutional value. The deictic expression *March 13, 2007* delimits the temporal context of the Bill to a one-day event, leaving the non-specialist without any chance of gaining pragmatic knowledge about the timeline of the Bill. Both the spatial and temporal localisations further point to the deictic centre (origo) identified with *Mr Oberstar*, and the reader is expected to recall knowledge about this person. The vague information provided by the absolute social deictics *Mr.* and *Ms.* only attach a high social status to *Oberstar* and *Johnson*. The use of the proximate person deictic *himself* points vaguely to *Oberstar* as being more important than *Johnson* in relation to the deictic particle *the*, which denotes the specificity of the *following bill*. The verb *referred* is post-fixed with the deictic particle *to* which completes the meaning of the procedure by pointing to *Committee on Transportation and Infrastructure* as the recipient. Contextual information thus draws heavily on the reader's social and pragmatic schemata, which need to be retrieved for the correct contextualisation of the discourse.

In the corresponding mashed-up text, different semiotic resources were used in the social space for the same rhetorical purpose of spatial, temporal and social localisation as in examples (2-4):

(2)

In the House of Representatives =>
- Google map for observation of US Congress Buildings and Grounds
- Pinpointing to geospatial data on the House of Representatives
- Text popup hypermediated by the pin: *The House of Representatives meets in the south wing of the United States Capitol, and has done so since 1807*

(3)

March 13, 2007 =>
- Time Chart (see Table 3-1) with hypermedia links to related spatial coordinates
- Lines tracing the Bill itineraries between the starting and ending venues
- Red and green map pins: colour codes refer to itinerary directions and Bill status

1. The bill was referred to the Committee on Transportation and Infrastructure.	*3/13/07*
2. The bill was returned from Committee.	*4/19/07*
3. The bill passed the House by a recorded vote of 394 to 25 and went to the Senate for consideration.	*4/19/07*
4. The bill passed the Senate by a recorded vote of 91 to 4 and went to the President.	*5/16/07*
5. The President vetoed the bill and returned it to the House.	*11/2/07*
6. The veto override passed the House by a recorded vote of 361 to 54 and went to the Senate for consideration.	*11/06/07*
7. The veto override passed the Senate by a recorded vote of 79 to 14 and the bill became law.	*11/8/07*

Table 3-1 Mashed-up Chart: Temporal Localisation of the Bill (H.R. 1495)

(4)
Mr. Oberstar => Hypermedia popups with photos, informative texts with bullet points about the persons involved:

Sponsor:
• *Rep. Oberstar [James Oberstar, Democrat, Minnesota, 18 Terms, Sworn in 1975]*

Cosponsors:
- *Rep. Mica [John Mica, Republican, 7th District, Florida, 11th Term, Sworn in 1993]*
- *Rep. Baker [Richard Baker, Republican, Louisiana, 11 Terms, Sworn in 1987]*
- *Rep. Johnson [Eddie Johnson, Democrat, 30th District, Texas, 11th Term, Sworn in 1993]*

Example (2) shows how the reader no longer relies only on the written Bill text, but can create new social knowledge through visual language, or "[…] the tight coupling of words, images, and shapes into a unified communication unit" (Horn 1999: 27). Readers can process geospatial information as a resource of place semiotics (Scollon / Scollon 2003), and couple it with iconic and textual information to self-construct the spatial meaning of social discourse.

In Example (3), the numbered sentences and the related dates generated in the tertiary text in Table 3-1 provide explicit temporal localisation of the stages the Bill has undergone to become a law. The diachronic chart also co-exists with coloured geospatial information (blue lines, red and green pins) to create social discourse continuity. Readers can thus easily self-construct pragmatic knowledge about the Bill in the rhetorical unit actually operated by the text and the images.

In Example (4), a rhetorical unit is this time operated by photos and short informative texts with bullet points which clearly specify:

a. *social identity*: e.g. Oberstar's first name is James, works in Minnesota, and is pictured as a middle-aged white man;
b. *social relations*: e.g. Mica, Baker and Johnson are in a sponsor-cosponsor relationship with Oberstar;
c. *pragmatic information*: e.g. the people proposing the Bill belong to the two major US political parties (Democratic and Republican); Oberstar was sworn in as a Congress member before the others and is serving in his 18th term in Congress. Bullet points postpone the original information load of *Mr. Oberstar* (*for himself and Ms. Eddie Bernice Johnson of Texas*)

by breaking the text into the chunks of sponsor and cosponsors.

Easification in the Professional and Tactical Spaces of Bills

Acculturation into the professional practice of drafting a Bill requires an understanding of its cognitive structuring, or "[…] the conventionalized and standardized organization used by almost all the members of the professional community […]" (Bhatia 1993: 32). Bill drafts are conventionally organised in the following parts: general rule, exceptions, special rules, transitional rules, other provisions, definitions and date. In this analysis, only the general rule was considered for its stated legislative intention, which addresses the layperson as in example (5):

(5)
To provide affordable, quality health care for all Americans and reduce the growth in health care spending, and for other purposes. (H.R. 3200)

This example illustrates how the keywords *provide*, *affordable*, *quality* and *reduce* are clear and cleverly positioned in the initial part of the statement to attract the reader's attention. Conversely, the vague expression *for other purposes* is tactically placed at the end without any further specification. This expression is part of the text's cognitive structuring which "[…] depends upon the communicative purpose(s) that it serves in the genre […]" (Bhatia 1993: 32). Under-specification of the full legal purpose may sometimes render professional discourse opaque with the ultimate aim of maintaining power and control.

Mashed-up texts, however, afford a hypertextual link to OpenCongressorg, a non-specialist legal community of practice. Here, pertinent information is provided in the form of tables containing official data, as shown in Table 3-2 for the case of H.R. Bill 3200.

Version	Word Count	Changes: Previous Version	Percent Change
Introduced in House	176,276	==	==
Reported in House	395,096	1,002	67%

Table 3-2 Statistical Data for the Cognitive Structuring of H.R. Bill 3200 (source: OpenCongress)

Data reveal statistical differences between the two versions of H.R. Bill 3200 due to the amendments made. In comparing the wording of the general rule in the two versions, the expression of legislative intent *for other purposes* was found to carry no indication of [*strike out all after*] as in many other parts of the Bill. This confirms that the real legislative intent is deliberately vague in spite of the significant reduction in the word count.

Thus, the main rhetorical purpose of this device is to help the reader gain awareness of what is NOT the effective legislative intent of the Bill. This reasonable degree of awareness is further enhanced by a dynamic mashup affordance, which allows the reader to engage interactively with the original Bill and *rollover any line of text to comment it*. Examples (6-10) show the comments that were aggregated in the mashed-up text related to the legislative intent of H.R. Bill 3200:

> (6)
> *It is my understanding that this bill is addressing the lack of health care and/or insurance coverage for 47 out of 300+ million people in this country. This number includes people who are sufficiently wealthy to elect not to sign up for health insurance; those who have not signed up for Medicare, Medicaid, or similar federal/state programs. In short, these 47 million people are covered. This bill is neither mandated nor even necessary. Please define "and for other purposes" or remove this phrase from the bill.*

> (7)
> *Also, "quality health care" and "reduce the growth in health care spending" is an oxymoron. It is impossible to provide every single person in the United States with top quality health care AND reduce spending.*

> (8)
> *Also, reduce spending for who? The consumers, the government, the providers?*

> (9)
> *The bill could remove all concerns about "other purposes" if it were worded like "To provide affordable, quality health care for all American and reduce the growth in health care spending, and for other purposes described in this bill".*

> (10)
> *I agree that "and for other purposes" needs to be HEAVILY defined. This is the reading between the lines part that the government plans on us not catching so they can sneak in whatever other agenda they have.*

Examples (6-10) show how different non-specialists interact with the original text given in example (5) to produce a *hypergenre* (cf. Giltrow / Stein 2009), which incorporates the traditional genre of bills with a newly constructed genre negotiated in this particular medium. Mashup affordances, in fact, allow the readers to become co-authors of new discourses which point to the rhetorical practice of ensuring professional topic continuity. This practice subverts the "parameters for community formation" (Giltrow / Stein 2009: 10), allowing the non-specialists to engage in *social apprenticeship* in the legal community which is notorious for circumscribing its discourse. Within this wider community, *constitutive intertertextuality* (Fairclough 1995), or interdiscursivity, is co-authored with the shared communicative objective of providing helpful professional and socio-cultural information to clarify the legislative intent of the Bill.

In example (6), though the expression *it is my understanding* indicates that the information may be subjective, topic continuity is ensured through the provision of institutional figures (*47 out of 300+ million*) and references (*Medicare, Medicaid*), which introduce the socio-professional plea *please define* for clarification. This is further expanded in example (7) to the oxymoronic play between *quality health care* and *reduce the growth in health care spending* through the use of *also* for topic continuity, which introduces example (8) as well. Here, however, focus is placed on clarifying *who* is the beneficiary of reducing *spending* by referring to possible social categories (*the consumers, the government, the providers*). Subsequently, example (9) suggests rewording the legislative intent as *for other purposes described in this bill* in order to *remove all concerns*. Finally, example (10) expresses topic continuity with both the previous texts (*I agree*) and the original text (*and for other purposes*), while introducing a critical note *needs to be*, emphasised by *HEAVILY defined*. This is followed by the social warning *that the government plans on us not catching*, and raises awareness of the reason behind it (*so they can sneak in whatever other agenda they have*).

Easification in the Textual Space of Bills

Like other legal texts, bills are governed by the pragmatic principle of avoidance of ambiguity and precision of interpretation, resulting in text complexity (cf. Gotti 2012). In the left column of example (11), the lengthiest original sentence (79 words) found in the corpus is integrated with different hyperlinks, generated automatically by the mashup. These connect to the different popup informative texts presented in the right column of the same example. The reader can choose to consult any of the informative texts, which have the nonlinear rhetorical purpose of mediating syntactic and/or lexical complexity.

(11)

If the person sold, delivered, or otherwise transferred a handgun,	*A person who*
ammunition, semiautomatic assault weapon, or	*Assault weapon has the same meaning as a semiautomatic assault weapon (Federal Public Safety and Recreational Firearms Use Protection Act, 18 U.S.C. section 921(a)(30).*
large capacity ammunition feeding device	*A fixed or detachable device capable of accepting more than ten rounds of ammunition*
to a juvenile knowing or	*A young person under the legal age*
having reasonable cause to know that such person intended to carry or otherwise possess or discharge or otherwise use the handgun, ammunition, semiautomatic assault weapon, or large capacity ammunition feeding device in the	*Aware that*
commission of a crime of violence,	*Committing*
shall be fined,	*will be fined, imprisoned or both*
under this title, imprisoned for not more than 10 years, or both. (H.R. 227, Sec. 3. (B)(ii)).	*title 18 of this bill*

For the sake of precision, the adverbial clause (protasis), introduced by the conditional *If*, includes repetitive information (*otherwise, handgun, ammunition, semiautomatic assault weapon, or large capacity ammunition feeding device*) and functions as a finite adjunct to circumscribe conditions. The 64-word length of this dependent clause, however, causes information load and creates syntactic discontinuity with the 15-word main clause (apodosis). The *if*-condition clause is replaced in the first popup by the relative clause *who*, which makes the condition clearer without causing syntactic incompleteness in the remaining clause.

In the second popup, the reader notices the redundancy of *semiautomatic*, and is aware of the wider legislative context of the issue through the referential link to another legal text (*Federal Public Safety and Recreational Firearms Use Protection Act*). The opaque expression *large capacity ammunition feeding device* is subsequently clarified in the plain language of *accepting more than ten rounds of ammunition*. The definition for the borrowed word *juvenile* (Latin *juvenilis,* from *juvenis* young person) provides the legal functional meaning of *under the legal age* for the normal function of *juvenile* as *a young person*. The common adjective *reasonable* is devoid of exact meaning even when used in expressions such as *reasonable cause*. In this case, semantic vagueness is avoided through the use of the plain expression *aware that*. The obsolete nominalisation *in the commission of* is rendered in the common verbalised form of *committing*. The main clause is eventually introduced by the deontic modal verb *shall*, which expresses the imperative consequences deriving from the actions. Ambiguity with the normal function of *shall* as a marker of the future tense (cf. Crystal / Davy 1969) is avoided through the use of *will be*. In the same popup, the three consequential actions are also provided to avoid their syntactic discontinuity created by the qualification *under this title*. Here, vagueness is avoided through another link which clarifies the intra-textual reference made. This dynamic move between primary and secondary texts allows the reader to split intra- and intertextual meaning into smaller units to reduce information load and clarify cognitive structuring, and to proceed to self-constructing a meaningful tertiary text.

Concluding Remarks

Nowadays, the discursive practice of proposing a US Bill is paralleled with new practices performed in mashup environments by the non-specialist community to gain a better understanding of this specialised discourse.

This study has attempted to show the different ways in which specific mashups can function as non-linear rhetorical easification devices to make US bills more accessible to non-specialist readers. The multi-perspective analysis revealed that *place semiotics* and its *interdiscursive dialogicality* played a key role in helping the ordinary reader develop social and pragmatic knowledge in order to (re)contextualise the social discourse of bills. In the professional and tactical spaces, affordances allowed laypeople to interact with the original bill, and subsequently to create a non-specialist community, where hypergeneric discourse was mediated through *constitutive intertertextuality* for professional knowledge. In the textual space, hypertextual links between primary and secondary texts facilitated the reader's understanding of intra- and intertextual meaning and encouraged self-construction of tertiary texts through *vertical intertextuality*.

Overall, the mashed-up texts can be considered as informative versions without drastic changes made to the meaning of original bills. The interrelated semiotic systems which shape these texts easify bill discourse by developing non-specialist readers' awareness of how it operates within the multi-perspective spaces. Dynamic affordances allow non-specialists to consult informative semiotic resources to reduce information load and avoid text complexity, and to author their own versions for full discourse interpretation.

References

Bazerman, Charles 2004. Intertextuality: how texts rely on other texts. In Barzeman, C. / Prior, P. (eds.) *What Writing does and How it does it. An Introduction to Analyzing Texts and Textual Practices.* Mahwah, NJ: Lawrence Erlbaum: 83-96.

Beaufort, Anne 2000. Learning the trade: a social apprenticeship model for gaining writing expertise. *Written Communication* 17(2): 185-223.

Bhatia, Vijay K. 1983. Simplification v. Easification: the case of legal texts, *Applied Linguistics* 4(1): 42-54.

—. 1987. Textual-mapping in British legislative writing. *World Englishes*,6(1): 1-10.

—. 1993. *Analysing Genre: Language Use in Professional Settings.* London: Longman.

—. 1998. Intertextuality in legal discourse. *The Language Teacher Online* 22(11). http://jalt-publications.org/old_tlt/files/98/nov/bhatia

—. 2004. *Worlds of Written Discourse: A Genre-based View*. London: Continuum.

—. 2008. Genre analysis, ESP and professional practice. *English for Specific Purposes* 27: 161-174.

Bhatia, Aditi / Bhatia, Vijay K. 2011. Discursive illusions in legislative discourse: a socio-pragmatic study. *International Journal for the Semiotics of Law* 24: 1-19.

Blackledge, Adrian 2005. *Discourse and Power in a Multilingual World.* Amsterdam/Philadelphia: John Benjamins.

Boehme-Nessler, Volker 2010. *Pictorial Law: Modern Law and the Power of Pictures*. Berlin: Springer-Verlag.

Charnock, Ross 2006. Clear ambiguity. In Wagner, A. / Cacciaguidi-Fahy, S. (eds.) *Legal Language and the Search for Clarity: Practice and Tools*. Bern: Peter Lang: 65-104.

Crystal, David / Davy, Derek 1969. *Investigating English Style.* London: Longman.

Fairclough, Norman 1995. *Discourse and Social Change.* Cambridge: Polity Press.

—. 2003. *Analysing Discourse. Textual Analysis for Social Research.* London: Routledge.

Fairclough, Norman / Mulderrig, Jane / Wodak, Ruth 2011. Critical Discourse Analysis. In van Dijk, T.A. (ed.) *Discourse Studies. A Multidisciplinary Introduction* [2nd ed.]. London: Sage: 357-378.

Feigenson, Neal / Sherwin, Richard K. / Spiesel, Christina 2005. Law in the digital age: how visual communication technologies are transforming the practice, theory, and teaching of law. *NYLS Legal Studies Research Paper No. 05/06-6*, 1-58.

Fiske, John 1987. *Television Culture*. London: Methuen.

Gambaro, Antonio 2007. Interpretation of multilingual Legislative Texts. *Electronic Journal of Comparative Law*, vol. 11.3. <http://www.ejcl.org/113/article113-4.pdf>.

Giltrow, Janet / Stein, Dieter 2009. Genres in the Internet: innovation, evolution, and genre theory. In Giltrow, J. / Stein, D. (eds.) *Genres in the Internet: Issues in the Theory of Genre*. Amsterdam/Philadelphia: John Benjamins: 1-25.

Gotti, Maurizio 2012. Text and genre. In Tiersma, P. / Solan, L. (eds.) *The Oxford Handbook of Language and Law*. Oxford: Oxford University Press: 52-66.

Gunnarsson, Britte-Louise 2009. *Professional Discourse*. London: Continuum.

Horn, Robert E. 1999. Information design: emergence of a new profession. In Jacobson, R. (ed.) *Information Design*. Cambridge, MA: The MIT Press: 15-33.

Jensen, Klaus Bruhn 2003. Communicating models: the relevance of models for research on the worlds of the Internet. In Hjarvard, S. (ed.) *Media in a Globalized Society*. Copenhagen: Museum Tusculanum Press: 257-289.

Kress, Gunther R. / van Leeuwen, Theo 2001. *Multimodal Discourse: The Modes and Media of Contemporary Communication*. London: Edward Arnold.

Lamb, Brian 2007. Dr. Mashup; or, why educators should learn to stop worrying and love the remix. *Educause Review* 42(4): 12-25.

Levinson, Stephen C. 2004. Deixis. In Horn, L.R. / Ward, G. (eds.) *The Handbook of Pragmatics*. Oxford: Blackwell: 97-121.

Marmaridou, Sophia S.A. 2000. *Pragmatic Meaning and Cognition*. Amsterdam/Philadelphia: John Benjamins.

Navas, Eduardo 2010. Regressive and reflexive mashups in sampling culture. In Sonvilla-Weiss, S. (ed.) *Mashup Cultures*. Wien: Springer-Verlag: 157-177.

Orna-Montesinos, Concepción 2012. *Constructing Professional Discourse. A Multiperspective Approach to Domain-Specific Discourses.* Newcastle upon Tyne: Cambridge Scholars Publishing.

Plastina, Anna Franca 2012. *Applied Linguistics and Semantic Web Apps: Cases of Mediated Discursive Practices*. München: LINCOM.

Scollon, Ronald / Scollon, Susie Wong 2003. *Discourses in Place: Language in the Material World.* New York: Routledge.

Sherwin, Richard K. 2011. *Visualizing Law in the Age of the Digital Baroque: Arabesques & Entanglements.* New York: Routledge.

Slapper, Gary / Kelly, David 2001. *Sourcebook on the English Legal System.* [2nd ed.]. London: Cavendish.

Thibault, Paul J. 1991. *Social Semiotics as Praxis: Text, Social Meaning Making, and Nabokov's Ada*. Minneapolis: University of Minnesota Press.

van Dijk, Teun A. 2004. Discourse, knowledge and ideology. In Pütz, M. / Neff, J. / van Dijk, T.A. (eds.), *Communicating Ideologies. Multidisciplinary Perspectives on Language, Discourse and Social Practice*. Frankfurt: Peter Lang: 5-38.

Yu, Jin / Benatallah, Boualem / Casati, Fabio / Daniel, Florian 2008. Understanding mashup development. *IEEE Internet Computing* 12(5): 44–52.

CHAPTER FOUR

EXPERT TO LAY COMMUNICATION: LEGAL INFORMATION AND ADVICE ON THE INTERNET

JUDITH TURNBULL

Introduction

In any specialised field there is a strong knowledge asymmetry between the expert and the layperson. In the case of the law, this gap is accentuated by its syntactic complexity, highly technical vocabulary and specialised register, as much as the technical content and procedural knowledge of the discipline. No matter how directly and personally a problem may concern the layperson, he or she will most probably feel the need for the assistance of an expert. However, the advent of the Internet has changed the way people communicate and the way they interact with institutions. Such an abundance of information of all kinds is now available online that more and more people, especially with the high cost of professional help and advice, are adopting a do-it-yourself approach to problem solutions by searching for information on their own, especially in the medical and legal fields. This chapter aims to investigate the characteristics of this type of discourse on the Internet and to see what strategies are used in the transfer of legal expertise to the layperson.

The subject of this study is the British government's website, direct.gov.uk, which provides ordinary citizens with access to public sector services in addition to information about the law and people's rights. Over the last twenty years, the plain language movement has called for more comprehensible legal texts and campaigned against the use of legalese, jargon and gobbledygook in public communication to enable ordinary people "to understand what they were doing when they had to, say, fill in a tax form" (Williams 2004: 116). The focus of this paper therefore straddles two areas of concern, as it will consider the transfer of expert legal information and advice as well as public communication on the British government's website.

Numerous studies have examined the features of legal discourse that give rise to its complexity (Charrow / Charrow 1979; Williams 2005; Gotti 2005). These characteristics will be taken into consideration in the current analysis to see what kinds of strategies are adopted to facilitate the understanding of a technical legal question. As far as public communication is concerned, early work in Critical Discourse Analysis (CDA) observed its 'conversationalization', which consisted in "the modelling of public discourse upon the discursive practices of ordinary life" (Fairclough 1994: 243), with the risk of what Fairclough called "synthetic personalization" (1993: 141). Other studies have identified culture-specific differences in comparative analyses of public administration discourse (Scott and Power 1994, Lavid 2000, Turnbull forthcoming), and shown that public discourse in the UK tends to be much more informal and friendly than in other countries. In particular, studies in expert-lay communication have focused on the popularisations of science (Myers 2003; Calsamiglia and van Dijk 2004; Ciapuscio 2003) and medical situations (Gülich 2003) and, despite their different scope, both studies provide insights for an analysis in the legal field.

The specific legal topic considered here is divorce, an increasingly common situation in which an ordinary citizen may well be tempted to seek information online by googling a query. Numerous websites have been set up by law firms or online divorce businesses which have an immediate commercial interest in providing enough information to attract new clients. By contrast, legal information and advice on Directgov is given in a disinterested manner as the objective of the website is purely to provide access to specialised information and expertise.

Corpus and Methodology

The corpus selected for this study is made up of two parts. The first is the law on divorce, the *Matrimonial Causes Act 1973* (31,144 words), which obviously serves as the point of reference for legal advice and information on the matter. This will be used for comparison with the second part of the corpus made up of all the web pages concerning divorce from the direct.gov.uk website (18,303 words), together with the forms necessary to file for divorce available online and accompanying notes providing help with procedure and form completion.

As expert-lay communication "must always adapt to the appropriateness conditions and other constraints of the media and communicative events"

(Calsamiglia / van Dijk 2004: 371), particular attention is given to the context of the communication, its participants, their roles and positions, register, text type, communicative function and the channel of communication. This analysis therefore draws on a number of approaches, both quantitative and qualitative, though primarily Discourse Analysis and Critical Discourse Analysis, in order to capture the complexity of the communicative event.

The Conditions and Constraints of Online Expert-lay Communication

The process of knowledge transfer involved in expert-lay communication is referred to by a variety of terms, such as popularisation, translation, transposition and re-contextualisation. All involve a simplification that remodels the language to suit the new target audience, so that it is close to general discourse and the lay public's everyday experiences (Gotti 2005: 205). Rewriting enables the reader to see the situation from his or her point of view, so that abstract knowledge is associated with familiar situations and becomes practical knowledge. A number of strategies are adopted to assist this transfer, including reformulation, illustration, description, scenarios, exemplification, metaphors and analogies, definitions, re-contextualisation, expansion, reduction and concretisation (Ciapuscio 2003; Gülich 2003; Calsamiglia / van Dijk 2004), though only a few of these are actually present on the website, as the analysis will show.

Expert-lay communication can take place with different levels of experience on the part of the layperson, from a total lack of knowledge to the position of a semi-layperson to a novice. It can also fulfil different purposes, whether it be in a professional context, in pedagogical settings for education at various levels (school or university), or simply for information and personal cultural development. The situation created on the website is an example of professional expert-lay communication, as between a lawyer and client, and therefore there is no attempt to 'teach' the law by presenting it in disciplinary terms and provide the reader with the 'secondary culture' (Widdowson 1979 cited in Gotti 2005: 204). It aims simply to be informative. However, it also differs from popularisations of science, for example, which seek to transfer abstract, scientific knowledge, often very distant from the world of the layperson, in order to broaden the reader's general knowledge. In fact, the communicative function of the web pages is to give practical and pragmatic advice to enable a person to find his or her way through the difficult process of a divorce.

Online expert-lay communication acquires some unusual and complicating characteristics. Firstly, it is not one-to-one communication, but one-to-many and 'the many' are not an online community with a common level of shared knowledge. They are an unknown, undefined and certainly heterogeneous public, heterogeneous in the sense of family background, life experiences, culture and education, especially bearing in mind that Britain today is a truly multicultural society, and as a consequence there may even be quite different levels of linguistic competence. This makes it difficult to define the level of shared cultural, institutional and 'world' knowledge and adjust the rewriting accordingly (van Dijk 2005). Secondly, the channel itself influences how information is presented through hypertext, which organises information into small, independent, self-contained pages in a similar way to a narrative structure which divides a 'story' into chunks and orders events in time in a logical and predictable sequence, what Chafe refers to as sub-chunking (quoted in Stewart 2004: 125). These chunks in hypertexts are divided first into pages and then into sections or paragraphs, thus filtering and streamlining information, perhaps even diluting it. Thirdly, although it is written text, the immediacy and the intimacy of the channel with the reader (probably sitting comfortably in his/her own home with apparent control over what he/she reads) lend themselves to a more direct and less formal approach.

Analysis

The channel of communication

Any analysis of a website must necessarily consider semiotic aspects, such as layout, colour and textual organisation, as they all contribute to the text, its message and, most importantly, the relationship with the reader (Kress / van Leeuwen 2001: 20). The most immediate aspect of the web pages under examination is the rather surprising use of orange as the framing colour. As the web pages are contained in the direct.gov.uk website, red or blue might have been expected for a British government website.

The homepage has the familiar and typical triptych layout of most websites. The main body contains the information specific to the page, whilst the left hand column gives an overview of the whole website with links to the other sections and the right hand column provides links to other important pages connected with the main topic of the web page. Users are guided to the information they are seeking by a number of indexical pages which gradually zoom in on the information required. It is interesting to note that many of the headings indicating the content of links or the various paragraphs on the page do not use nouns and prefer the verbal *–ing* form, as for example, *Planning and getting a divorce, Looking after children if you divorce or separate* and *Completing your divorce and getting a decree absolute*, thus signalling the action to be taken by the user. Each page is then broken down into a number of paragraphs, each with a heading at the top and a 'label' on the right hand side of the main column made up of a phrase or even a whole sentence taken from the text in order to focus the user's attention on the core idea of each section or paragraph. Thus these headings and subheadings give users toeholds in scaling the information provided on the website.

Potentially a website offers new and innovative ways of presenting information through its multi-modality. However, visuals and other graphical elements are kept to a minimum and there is only one small image per page which fails to illustrate useful points in the text, but is purely symbolic or vaguely representative of the information given on the page. For example, a photograph of a pen lying on a piece of printed paper appears on the page called "Legal agreements if you split up or separate". Only one concession to multi-modality is made in the form of a video in which a family talks about their painful experiences of divorce and how they have overcome them.

Comparison between the law and website information

To appreciate fully the changes that take place in the rewriting of the legal information contained in the law for the purposes of the website, it will be useful to first give a brief outline of the main features of legal discourse, both written and spoken, and then compare extracts from the Act and the website with the equivalent information. The main characteristics of legal discourse, as adapted from Williams (2004) and Charrow / Charrow (1979), can be summarised as follows:

i. archaic or rarely used words or expressions
ii. foreign words and expressions, especially from Latin
iii. repetition of words expressions and syntactic structures
iv. long, complex sentences, with intricate patterns of coordination and subordination
v. frequent use of passive constructions
vi. highly impersonal style of writing
vii. tendency towards nominalisation

Three examples will suffice to give an indication of how the 'translation' is made. In example 1, the short extract from the law contains a negative, a passive, a nominalisation and the modal 'shall', which has caused much debate in the plain language movement. All of these contribute to its most significant characteristic – its highly impersonal and abstract style. By contrast, the website version shows a re-contextualisation, or repositioning of the discourse in that the subject is no longer divorce, but rather potential divorcees addressed directly as *you and your husband or wife*, immediately involving the user.

Example 1

Law	Website
Bar on petitions for divorce within one year of marriage. (1) No petition for divorce shall be presented to the court before the expiration of the period of one year from the date of the marriage	To file for divorce, you and your husband or wife will need to: have been married for at least a year (two years in Northern Ireland)

The next example clearly demonstrates the complexity of the legislative text with a subordinate structure in paragraph 2, presenting a negative proposition introduced by the modal 'shall not' and followed by the negative conditional *unless*, thus making the sentence a double negative. The two negatives resolve to a positive, but as Charrow / Charrow (1979: 1324-5) point out, multiple negatives, especially in subordinate or embedded clauses, can create more comprehension problems. On the website, however, the same legal point has been completely rewritten in the positive form to avoid the complicated negatives and thus facilitate understanding.

Example 2

Law	Website
1 Divorce on breakdown of marriage. (1) Subject to section 3 below, a petition for divorce may be presented to the court by either party to a marriage on the ground that the marriage has broken down irretrievably. (2) The court hearing a petition for divorce shall not hold the marriage to have broken down irretrievably unless the petitioner satisfies the court of one or more of the following facts, that is to say— ………	Understand grounds for divorce You can only divorce if your marriage has 'irretrievably broken down'. You will need to prove this to the court by giving the reasons your marriage has ended. These are known as 'facts' for divorce. Find out what reasons ('grounds') you can give that your marriage should end.

It is also interesting to note how the term 'grounds' has been 'translated' into *reasons*, accompanied by the original form highlighted in both inverted commas and brackets to make sure the reader makes the connection between the two.

In example 3 below the Act has one sentence of 88 words, with complex embedding of clauses to define the situation in which the spouse who did not start the divorce may apply for the decree absolute. The very verbose and roundabout explanation of the law is rewritten and broken down into chunks on the website, with short sentences and simple, explicit direct information. An introductory sentence to the question is given to explain clearly what the matter is and then two different situations are hypothesised in simple terms, whether *you* or *your husband or wife* started the divorce.

Similarly, the time specification is simplified to make it as comprehensible as possible, so that "at any time after the expiration of three months from the earliest date on which that party could have made such an application", becomes "the earliest you can apply is 3 months, six weeks and a day".

Example 3

Law	Website
9 Proceedings after decree nisi: general powers of court. …. (2) Where a decree of divorce has been granted and no application for it to be made absolute has been made by the party to whom it was granted, then, at any time after the expiration of three months from the earliest date on which that party could have made such an application, the party against whom it was granted may make an application to the court, and on that application the court may exercise any of the powers mentioned in paragraphs (a) to (d) of subsection (1) above.	When you can apply for a decree absolute depends on whether you or your husband or wife started the divorce. If you started the divorce You can apply to the court for a decree absolute – but you must wait six weeks and a day after the decree nisi was issued. If your husband or wife started the divorce If you want to apply for a decree absolute but your husband or wife started the divorce, you have to wait an additional three months. So the earliest you can apply is three months, six weeks and a day after the decree nisi was issued.

These three examples indicate some of the general characteristics of the website text – personalisation, simplification at a structural and syntactic level and the breaking down of information into accessible chunks, which all form part of the strategy of "concretization", a procedure defined by Gülich as "rewording abstract information in a non-abstract manner" (2003: 244). This seems to be the main strategy adopted. It is interesting to note the total absence of metaphor in the text, even though metaphor is often considered one of the most important and effective mechanisms for explanation and illustration (Gülich 2003: 241; Gotti 2005: 206). However, as Gülich (2003: 245) points out, procedures of concretisation make it much easier for the layperson to 'connect' the information to their everyday lives than the complicated use of metaphors. The following paragraphs will investigate these points more closely.

Personalisation

The informal and personal style of communication on the website is marked by an overwhelming use of the second person pronoun *you* to address the reader directly. The frequency list drawn up by ConcApp software showed that *you* was not only the first content word with 1139 occurrences (6.2230%), but also the very first word in the list, even above grammatical words such as *to*, *the* or *a*. In addition, active verb forms which take the user as subject and are sometimes imperative predominate, indicating what action should be taken and thus putting the user into the driving seat, so to speak, as in examples (1) to (4):

(1) Find out how the divorce process works, what you'll need to do and how long it can take.
(2) Find out when you can manage your own divorce – and how to do it.
(3) You can find out more about how to apply for a financial order by following the link below.
(4) You may think solicitors will have to do a lot of work for you when you're divorcing. But in many cases, you can handle most of the arrangements yourselves.

Often a 'scenario' is presented in which a possible situation, event or reaction is illustrated by the expert and a selection of alternative actions are proposed so that the addressee can evaluate them and act accordingly (Gülich 2003: 244), a strategy often adopted (examples (5) to (7)):

(5) If you haven't managed to reach an agreement before you go to the solicitors, they will try to arrange one for you.
(6) If you're finding it difficult to agree about how to look after children or split up your property and possessions, using a mediator can save you time and money.
(7) If you're able to agree everything with your spouse, you won't have to attend any court hearings.

Features of informal style present in the website include the use of *they* to avoid the heavy repetition of *he/she* and *him/her*. This use of the plural pronoun to refer back to a singular subject may not be considered as grammatically correct by all, and it therefore gives a sense of informality in legal discourse (examples (8) and (9)):

> (8) A mediator is an independent person who will work with both of you to reach an agreement. They won't take sides and will keep your discussions confidential.
> (9) Your husband or wife can agree the divorce or they can argue against ('defend') it. They will show this when they fill in their form D10.

There is an almost total absence of archaic or foreign words, which are characteristic of legal discourse (the only exceptions are *affidavit* and *decree nisi*), in contrast with the use of many colloquialisms, thus reinforcing the connection with everyday life and experience:

> (10) It will speed things up if your spouse agrees with the reasons that you want to use.
> (11) Dealing with debts when you split up.
> (12) If the court is happy, it will send you both a form D37 (decree absolute).

And lastly, there are many emphatic expressions in the text that stress the emotional and psychological as well as practical aspects of divorce, and therefore underline the personal approach adopted in the website;

> (13) Every year thousands of families face the challenge of separation and divorce. But despite the pain and trauma, one thing everyone agrees on is that it's not our children's fault. Children shouldn't suffer as a result of their parents' separation and this is central to family mediation.
> (14) If you've agreed everything with your husband or wife, the divorce paperwork is usually quite straightforward.
> But if you are worried about filling the forms, you can get help from your local Citizens Advice Bureau.

Procedural language – simplification and sub-chunking

The concretisation and scenario strategies present the information and advice on a very practical plane, so much so that the text appears to take on the appearance of an operator's manual for a machine or electronic device of some kind, as "a narrative sequence of precisely defined actions that furnish a behavioural template on which the operator must model his or her actions" (Paradis 2004: 258). Similarly, the web pages give the behavioural template of how to operate a divorce. Paradis (2004: 266) names three rhetorical conventions that can be found in operational discourse:

1. Taxonomies or terminological standards
2. Conditional generalisations
3. Segmented action sequences.

According to Paradis (2004), all three conventions are concerned with accuracy and clarity, which are also obviously essential characteristics in legal information and advice. Taxonomies, or in our case legal terms, play an important role in the text by relating form to function and identifying the 'components' in the divorce process. In the context of knowledge transfer there is frequent switching from colloquial to technical language and vice versa (Gülich 2003: 240), though in the web pages they are reduced to a minimum with very few Latin terms and only a few highly specialised terms. In fact, they are just sufficient to establish some connection with the legal process (such as, *collaborative law*, *financial order*, *ancillary relief* and *consent order*), and are always accompanied by a definition to make absolutely clear to the user what they mean. Thus, in:

(15) 'Collaborative law'
Some solicitors use a process called 'collaborative law' when helping people to formally end their relationships. You, your partner and your solicitors meet together to reach an agreement. If you use solicitors this way, you will sign an agreement that you'll resolve your problems without going to court. There's no fixed timescale – your solicitors will work with you until you've made all the arrangements you need.
(16) A financial order (sometimes referred to as an 'ancillary relief order') is a formal arrangement made in court. Financial orders confirm agreements about money or property between a couple who are ending a marriage or a civil partnership.
(17) Form D80 is an 'affidavit' (a sworn statement) concerning your divorce. It confirms that what you say in your divorce petition is true. You must get this form witnessed by a member of court staff or a solicitor before submitting it to the court.

Conditional generalisations seek to establish circumstantial limits so that the tool is operated effectively and safely. In part, these limits are imposed externally by the constraints set by the divorce procedure, but the website also channels behaviour in certain directions to simplify and clarify the process. It therefore stresses the need to find an agreement with the ex-partner first of all or, alternatively, look for mediation if necessary and finally, use solicitors as a last resort. Furthermore, as we saw in examples (5), (6) and (7), the scenario strategy offers alternative actions for the addressee. In the website text, where the options are usually limited, the consequence will be for such text to always steer the reader towards some predetermined behaviour by clearly specifying and defining the either/or options open to the divorcees in certain circumstances:

(18) Divorcing without using solicitors
You may think solicitors will have a lot of work for you when you're divorcing. But in many case, you can handle most of the arrangements yourselves. Find out when you can manage your own divorce – and how to do it.

(19) If you want to meet the mediator alone, the mediator will ask you for your husband, wife or civil partner's contact details before the meeting. The mediator will contact them to find out if they are willing to try mediation. If they don't want to try mediation, you won't have to attend the meeting. If they agree to meeting the mediator, you will be able to meet the mediator alone.

Lastly, the segmented action sequences are the series of actions in steps through time to operate the device safely and successfully, and similarly the divorce process is resolved into a series of discrete operations to guide the divorcee through the procedure. First, a page lists the various stages of a divorce, establishing the grounds for divorce, reaching a settlement about children and possessions, filing the divorce petition obtaining a decree nisi and finally the decree absolute, and then each phase is dealt with in a separate page with the 'instructions for use' at each stage. The instructions are not given in the form of imperatives, but make an extensive use of modals, especially *can*, *may*, *need to*, *should*, thus presenting them in the form of advice and suggestions rather than as commands (Palmer 2001; Koester 2002; Portner 2007). In fact, there are just 18 instances of *must* and 12 of *have to*, in contrast with the 59 occurrences of *need to* and 31 for *should*:

(20) The form D10 must be returned to the court within eight days of you receiving it.

(21) You should try to decide how you will look after your children after you've divorced. You'll also need to be able to agree on where the children will live and how often your spouse will be able to see them.

Although both *need to* and *should* express a kind of obligation or necessity, they are gentler forms and appropriate for the setting of the website where advice and help are being given and the addresser wants to establish a friendly and relaxed relationship with the addressee. It is also interesting to notice the low frequency of negatives on the website (*not* 0.3060% and *no* 0.1093%) as opposed to the law itself (*not* 0.5330% and *no* 0.1156%), focussing on what should be done and how and therefore adopting a more proactive approach.

Moving from information to action

As the website emphasises the point that it is possible to divorce without the help of a solicitor on a number of occasions, the petition forms and the supporting notes for guidance are particularly important. In fact, the forms and notes follow in the same vein as the information on the website. At times a more formal style is used, as for example. *enter into a religious marriage*, but generally the language is simple, with non-technical vocabulary and straightforward sentence structures.

Once again there is an intensive use of *you* in the notes with 162 occurrences (4.0652 %) and the imperative. And yet, in contrast with these characteristics, we do find some technical points, as for example, the difference between *habitual residence* and *domicile,* which are explained rather vaguely despite being complex legal concepts. Particularly striking is the use of the highly technical term, *prayer*, which is specific to petitions and means the case a party of the prosecution brings before the court, or as defined in the notes, "your request to the court", and could be easily confused because of its completely different meaning in everyday usage. This clearly reflects deep-rooted tradition in the law and legal procedure which, regardless of the new channel of communication and the technological environment, maintains the rituals of court proceedings.

Discussion

Given that knowledge asymmetry creates an imbalance in the power relations between the two parties involved and that the communication we are interested in is taking place on an institutional website, it is appropriate to briefly consider the question from a Critical Discourse Analysis approach.

The purpose of the direct.gov.uk website is to inform citizens about their rights and responsibilities, thus empowering them to make decisions and take action. As we have seen, the prospective divorcee is 'told' how to approach the legal procedure through the use of scenarios which steer him/her through the various stages. Technical or semi-technical terms, with clear definitions, are used in the text to help 'connect' to the legal system and the court procedures, all of which is done in an intensely personal style with the reader being addressed directly. The advice in the form of suggestions reduces the imposition on the reader and therefore appears to narrow the gap between expert and layperson. However, the authorial voice of the expert remains anonymous throughout the web pages and the only explicit references to experts are in the third person:

> (22) Solicitors can help you end a relationship. They will negotiate with your partner (usually through their solicitor) and try to reach an agreement.

As a result, he remains aloof, giving the impression that the suggestions and advice come from a distant superior authority, thereby reinforcing the knowledge asymmetry and undermining the personalisation.

Legal procedures and legal discourse are complicated and certainly a world apart from the lay public. "As the differential between expertise and common sense becomes greater, or as the audience itself becomes more diverse, the demands made upon the operator's manual increase" (Paradis 2004: 258). The audience of a website is unknown and extremely diverse. Paradis (2004: 259) argues that texts can circulate expertise to masses, but the inherent rigidity of written discourse, coupled with the necessary reduction of complex situations to sequential units of simple action, increase the possibility of omission, ambiguity and misunderstanding. This means the advice given is often very general and at times, significantly, impersonal as it cannot accommodate the very individual and specific situations that readers face:

> (23) Going through this process will take time and cost you money. If it's possible, it's a very good idea to try and settle things between yourselves.
> (24) If you really can't agree arrangements about children when a relationship ends, one or both parents can apply to a court. This should be your last resort – taking these issues to court can be very difficult for you and your children.
> (25) It's important to bear in mind that defending a divorce can:
> - Take up a lot of time
> - Be very distressing
> - Lead to very high legal costs.

Indeed, the discrepancy or gap between situational complexities and discursive reduction can lead to an oversimplification. To compensate for this, we can find rather simplistic spelling out of points. This involves even some everyday expressions being defined or explained:

(26) You must cancel or 'freeze' any joint credit cards, store cards or bank accounts immediately when you know you will be divorcing or separating. When a bank or credit card company 'freezes' your account, it means no more money can be spent or taken out.
(27) A decree absolute is the legal document that ends your marriage. Once you have a decree absolute, you are divorced, no longer married and free to marry again if you wish.

At times simplification tends towards dumbing down:

(28) Sorting out the basics about possessions
Start by working out what both of you will need when you're living separately When you're divorcing or ending your civil partnership, you can usually sort out who will keep which possessions yourselves.
In general terms, it's a good idea to start by working out what both of you will need when you're living separately. For example, you'll both need a bed, sofa, and some kitchen equipment.
If you haven't got enough to share equally – for example, you may only have one sofa – you can make other arrangements. One of you might keep the sofa, while the other may take an agreed amount of money from a savings account to buy another one.

In view of this simplification and dumbing down procedure, it is surprising that the web pages did not make use of visuals, such as flow charts to plot out the divorce process, rather than rely entirely on language in order to convert and convey the information in a practical and concrete manner. Law certainly does not lend itself easily to graphic representation, but more could have been made of the multi-modal potential of the website.

Texts can break down and reorganise the complex phenomenological reality of objects and events and these reductions are necessary distortions. They help to establish perspective in simplified points of view that clarify structure and purpose, yet they also hide deeper complexities (Paradis 2004: 264). Reductionism, by ignoring the vast differences in situations, enables the user to see the situation as a system and to manipulate it logically and learn how to go through the procedure. Reducing the selection process to a protocol, a manual, gives the layperson the impression of being invested with expert behaviour. However, this may lead one into thinking that divorce is simple and into a false sense of security. After all, higher level experts set the conditions of the divorce procedure and court proceedings and the layperson may be faced with situations in which he or she cannot understand the potential consequences of specific actions or decisions, in which case the empowering of citizens is seriously undermined or just an illusion.

References

Calsamiglia, Helena / van Dijk, Teun A. 2004. Popularization discourse and knowledge about the genome. *Discourse and Society* 15: 369-389.

Charrow, Robert P. / Charrow, Veda R. 1979. Making legal language understandable: a psycholinguistic study of jury instructions. *Columbia Law Review* 79(7): 1306-1374

Ciapuscio, Guiomar E. 2003. Formulation and reformulation procedures in verbal interactions between experts and (semi-)laypersons. *Discourse Studies* 5(2): 207-233.

Fairclough, Norman 1993. Critical Discourse Analysis and the marketisation of public discourse: the universities. *Discourse and Society* 4(2): 133-168.

—. 1994. Conversationalization of public discourse and the authority of the consumer. In Keat R.W. / Abercrombie N. (eds.) *The Authority of the Consumer*. New York: Routledge: 253-268.

Gotti, Maurizio 2005. *Investigating Specialized Discourse*. Bern: Peter Lang.

Gülich, Elisabeth 2003. Conversational techniques used in transferring knowledge between medical experts and non-experts. *Discourse Studies* 5(2): 235-263.

Koester, Almut J. 2002. The performance of speech acts in workplace conversations and the teaching of communication functions. *System* 30: 167-184.

Kress, Gunther R. / van Leeuwen, Theo 2001. *Multimodal Discourse. The Modes and Media of Contemporary Communication*. London: Arnold.

Lavid, Julia 2000. Cross-cultural variation in multilingual instructions: a study of speech act realization patterns. In Ventola, E. (ed.) *Discourse and Community: Doing Functional Linguistics*. Tübingen: Gunter Narr Verlag: 71-85.

Myers, Greg 2003. Discourse studies of scientific popularisation: questioning the boundaries. *Discourse Studies* 5(2): 265-279.

Palmer, Frank R. 2001. *Mood and Modality*. Cambridge: Cambridge University Press.

Paradis, James 2004. Text and action. The operator's manual in context and in court. In Bazerman C. / Paradis J. (eds.) *Textual Dynamics of the Professions. Historical and Contemporary Studies of Writing in Professional Communities*: 256-278. Also available at http://wac.colostate.edu/books/textual_dynamics/: accessed March 25, 2012.

Portner, Paul 2007. Imperatives and modals. *Natural Language Semantics* 15(4): 351-383.

Scott, Donia / Power, Richard (eds.) 1994. The characteristics of administrative forms in English, German and Italian. (Gist deliverable EV-1, LRE Project 062-09). Available at http://mcs.open.ac.uk/rp3242/papers/EVI-final.pdf (last accessed January 20, 2011).

Stewart, Ann H. 2004. The role of narrative structure in the transfer of ideas. The case study and management theory. In Bazerman C. / Paradis J. (eds.) *Textual Dynamics of the Professions. Historical and Contemporary Studies of Writing in Professional Communities*: 120-144. Also available at http://wac.colostate.edu/books/textual_dynamics/ (last accessed March 25, 2012).

Turnbull, Judith 2012. Communication styles in the public administration: a comparative analysis of Italian and British websites. *Annali del Dipartimento di Metodi e Modelli per l'Economia, Finanza e il Territorio 2010-2011*: 3-30.

van Dijk, Teun A. 2005. Contextual knowledge management in discourse production. A CDA perspective. In Wodak, R. / Chilton, P.A. (eds.) *A New Agenda in Critical Discourse Analysis: Theory, Methodology and Interdisciplinarity*. Amsterdam/Philadelphia: John Benjamins: 71-100.

Williams, Christopher 2004. Legal English and Plain Language: an introduction. *ESP Across Cultures* 1: 111-124.

—. 2005. *Tradition and Change in Legal English: Verbal Constructions in Prescriptive Texts*. Bern: Peter Lang.

PART II:

ISSUES OF AUTHORITY, POWER AND IDENTITY

CHAPTER FIVE

COMPETING DISCOURSES OF RESPECT IN A YOUNG OFFENDERS INSTITUTION EDUCATION DEPARTMENT

PAOLA BOCALE

Introduction

This chapter[1] explores discourses of respect in the Education Department of a Young Offenders Institution (YOI). Research has shown that prison staff find it difficult to feel respect for prisoners because these are individuals who have officially lost that same respect in society (Jenkins 1991; Butler 2008). Moreover, it is argued that the very nature of prison makes it difficult for those in charge to feel respect for their passive and not autonomous subjects (Miller 2001; Liebling 2004). Butler / Drake (2007), who conducted research on the concept of respect in adult prisons, note that the realities of the prison system, such as the authoritarian environment, the status of prisoners as criminals, the role of staff as wardens, and the treatment of prisoners as passive recipients of power, make it impossible for offenders to earn the respect of the prison staff.

While adopting some of the analytical views presented in the reviewed studies, this analysis aims at achieving a more nuanced and in-depth understanding of the dynamics and discourses of respect in custodial correctional settings. In particular, it is hypothesised that whereas uniformed staff working in the Education Wing employ an authoritative discourse of respect underpinned by a view of the prisoners as a uniform and monolithic group, teachers and other civilian staff working with the young offenders give voice to diverse perspectives on respect based on a

---

[1] The author gratefully acknowledges the assistance of a BP Centenary Research Bursary while conducting this research. I thank all my informants for their help. For inspiration, wisdom and scholarly example I thank Annabella Santolin and Paola Ferretti.

greater acknowledgement of the prisoners as individuals, capable of personal improvement and rehabilitation. One of the main purposes of the study is to provide helpful information for implementing restorative justice in prisons for young offenders.

Research Framework and Design

The research was conducted in a Young Offenders Institution (HMYOIX) in England. According to prison service records the inmate population of HMYOIX in spring 2012 was about 410 convicted men aged between 18 and 21. Most young offenders are serving sentences of between one and three years for offences such as possession of drugs with intent to supply, burglary and robbery.

In spring 2012, there were 17 teachers employed in the Education Wing of HMYOIX. In addition to the teachers, there are between six and eight civilian staff, including administrative staff and library staff working in the YOI Library. Finally, there are always at least six officers on duty in the Education Wing during normal teaching hours. This brings the total number of staff working in Education to around 30 people, including the prison officers. Interviews were conducted with four teachers, one library employee and one former officer who had been working in HMYOIX until his retirement earlier in the year. Data for this paper come from five of the six interviews.

Data collection method: self-narratives

Little, if any, research has been conducted to date to examine the concept of respect in YOIs. Given the elusive and variable nature of the term, it was decided to adopt a participant-generated approach to understanding respect in a Young Offender Institution. Data was collected by means of self-narratives with staff working in close contact with the young offenders. In the interviews, participants were asked to recall and describe episodes in their work in the YOI when they felt that someone really deserved respect, episodes when they thought they had earned the respect of others and episodes when they experienced the respect of others. This chapter is based on a qualitative analysis of these interviews.

Mandated respect: John, a retired prison officer

John[2] is in his early 60s and retired recently from working as a prison officer in HMYOIX.

Theme 1: *Society has certain principles, values and rules, and those who break the rules must be punished as severely as possible*

John avows 'society's norms and standards', both in terms of how his world is and in terms of his way of being in that world. This avowal is coupled with a celebration of authority and of the necessity of severe punishment to enforce society's rules and to keep the world in order. Whoever violates society's norms and values must be prepared to accept the consequences, hard as they may be. Harsh punishment deters crime and punishment in general should be severe enough for wrongdoers to realise what they have done and prevent them from reoffending:

> *if someone has murdered they should pay a penalty for that if someone steals if they have murdered or committed bodily harm they should pay a penalty for that* [….] *and likewise for any indiscretion or felony or any offence.*[3]

Underpinning John's worldview is the retributive justice model, which emphasises delivering appropriate punishment (just deserts) to the offenders. Retributive justice draws from the mentality of 'you reap what you sow', or 'an eye for an eye' (Krimsky / Simoncelli 2011) and this is evident in John's reasoning on what can work to prevent reoffending:

> *if someone has stolen your purse and taken 20 pounds in your purse they get you a new purse and they pay you back double what they took.*

In discussing restorative justice, John completely discards the possibility that it may work to rehabilitate offenders and he does not consider it effective in preventing reoffending.

Theme 2: *Respect, as one of shared society's values, implies a personal involvement with and recognition of each other's individuality, and this is not possible in prison*

---

[2] Participants' names have been changed to protect their anonymity.

[3] Throughout the study, quotes have been edited to omit repetition and remove discourse fillers.

John places respect among the values shared by society's members, acknowledging the fact that *obviously a human being is respected.* What emerges from his line of argument about respecting prisoners is that respect implies a personal involvement with the individual and *you can't go on an individual basis* in prison. It is something of a paradox that in a coercive custodial institution such as a prison, where prisoners are continuously watched and scrutinised as they perform the most basic functions from personal hygiene to eating or even sleeping, they are at the same time not really looked at, or more precisely, as John puts it, they need not be looked at individually because that hinders the enforcement of security and discipline.

Theme 3: *A person's background and education determine that individual's future behaviour and attitudes, including their attitude towards respect*

John is strongly convinced that social attitudes and behaviours are the product of an individual's background and education, and as such should be taught at an early age. The implications of believing that social behaviour is taught to children in their early childhood is that if you have not been taught certain attitudes early it is very unlikely that you will learn them later on. It comes as no surprise that John is opposed to restorative justice and rehabilitative punishment, because the very idea of the possibility of transformation and change of an individual conflicts with his deterministic view of childhood as the stage when the future development of a human being is ultimately decided upon.

Theme 4: *There is a lamentable tendency nowadays to punish offenders not effectively enough*

The last theme running through John's interview stems logically from the first. As we saw earlier, John advocates the necessity of hard, even physical punishment for those who break society's norms, rules and values and remembers the old days when corporal punishment was allowed:

> *it's not that long ago in the sixties they still used to have birching the fact is that anyone who was birched hardly ever came back for a second dose because they'd learnt the lesson.*

Regretfully, in John's eyes, that is not the direction things are going in these days and John explicitly criticises what he considers contemporary tendencies to justify offenders for what they have done.

John considers the rehabilitation and re-education of young offenders as both a waste of money and an injustice to the victims and their families. In John's deterministic and ultimately pessimistic view of human behaviour, as moulded once and for all in a person's formative years, there is no place for later changes, and even if there were, that would not be desirable because it is unfair to victims, and to society, that offenders are rehabilitated.

John's discourse of respect

John's talk is shaped by an authoritative discourse that is not defined by an engagement with individual selves but only by an engagement with an institution, the prison. He repeatedly transforms the reality of prisoners as individuals into common-sense assumptions and depictions and oversimplified explanations about how to behave with offenders. A particularly striking instance of such formulaic thinking is John's insistence that officers cannot see prisoners as individuals because this only creates problems. Prisoners have to comply with the prison rules and regulations, whatever they are, and this is the only way they can get a certain degree of respect from the officers. Following Bakhtin (1981), the discourse of obedience can be considered an authoritative discourse that creates uniform understandings and flattens out contradictions, ambiguities and uncertainties.

Foucault investigated the practices and techniques for gradually bringing individuals in line with social norms and forms of behaviour, a process he termed normalisation (Foucault 1980). Prisons, schools and mental hospitals are examples of institutions involved in normalising perceived deviance from accepted norms through enforcement of a complex body of rules that are progressively internalised by their recipients until they modify their conduct accordingly. The ultimate purpose of the process of normalisation is to have individuals who are docile, obedient and compliant with society's rules and demands. The power of normalisation is imposed not only physically but, even more importantly, psychologically and culturally. Authoritarian discourses of respect as obedience and deference contribute powerfully to the regulation and normalisation of individuals in coercive institutions.

Respect is reciprocal: Mark, an English teacher

Mark is in his late fifties, teaches mostly English and Literacy but occasionally covers classes in most other subjects.

Theme 1: *Respect involves interaction and mutual understanding*

Contrary to John, the prison officer who refuses to interact with prisoners because he feels that this can be a threat to security and discipline, what emerges from the interview with Mark is that respect involves interaction and mutual understanding:

> *I suppose is just more understanding both sides so the prisoners need to understand our role and the officers' roles.*

The best way of dealing with prisoners in conflicting situations is to have a dialogue where each of the parties becomes reciprocally aware of the other's actions and expectations. Mark is not afraid of sharing his opinions with the offenders and opening up to their perspectives and believes in the role of communication in resolving conflict. Building a dialogue through interaction and understanding is one of the primary ways in which respect can be established.

The importance of building a dialogue among conflicting parties is emphasised in restorative justice and it comes as no surprise that Mark views restorative intervention as a positive step towards the rehabilitation of prisoners.

Theme 2: *Respect is a reciprocal relationship*

The second theme emerging from the interview with Mark is that respect is a reciprocal disposition which means that both parties are giving, or are prepared to give, something to each other:

> *there's no way you are going to have them to respect you if you are going to disrespect them.*

The practice of belittling and demeaning the offenders, which is carried out by some officers, has the effect of triggering conflict, because *if you belittle the prisoners they'll fight back* says Mark. Respect is thus a reciprocal association – you can only get it if you are willing to give it to others.

Theme 3: *Prisoners' respect as power and social status*

Physical strength, material possessions and extraordinary achievements are considered by the young offenders as bases for respect. Offenders achieve respect if they impose themselves over their opponents in a fight, if they show their strength and stereotypical macho behaviour and attributes, such as physical combativeness, muscles and tattoos. Material possessions work as symbols of personal worth and status and are key to both self-respect and respect from others. Outstanding, uncommon or remarkable achievements, such as some extraordinary crimes, ensure that respect "*in some cases is a perverse kind of respect based on having done some extraordinary crime*".

Respect based on extraordinary achievements somehow seems to contrast with the drive to respect conformity and sameness we discussed earlier. Hornsey / Jetten (2004) explain this paradox as based on the conflict between two different human needs: the need to belong and the need to affirm one's individuality. Young offenders respect those who yield to group values and expectations but at the same time acknowledge the exceptionality of those individuals who go on to become someone who stands out from the crowd, and not only in a negative sense. During the course of this research it was noted that, notwithstanding the widely held view that young offenders' disdain educational and cultural achievements, those few offenders who do have some sort of university background definitely benefit from a certain standing and esteem among their fellow inmates. And staff and visitors to the prison are often shown Level 1 and Level 2[4] qualifications by the offenders who have just achieved them in prison. These observations counteract the often reported stereotyped image of young offenders as individuals scorning education and the educated.

Mark's discourse of respect

Contrary to John, who refuses to acknowledge prisoners' individuality, Mark invokes a discourse of recognition of the offenders as individuals, worthy of respect and capable of rehabilitation. He constructs a discourse of personal relationship with the young offenders as one of commitment to finding a common ground for understanding and building a rapport despite the challenging nature of the prison environment.

[4] Qualifications offered at HMYOIX include OCR Adult Literacy and Numeracy Level 1 and Level 2.

Respect you earn: Anne, an Entry Level Literacy Teacher

Anne is in her early thirties, formerly a teacher in comprehensive schools in London, teaching entry level Literacy in HMYOIX.

Theme 1: *You earn respect*

Anne believes that she, as a teacher, must earn prisoners' respect. Earning the offenders' respect does not mean being rigid or acting in an authoritarian way any more than it involves being tough or inflexible or resorting to disciplinary practices. It means advocating civilised standards of conduct and not deviating from them. It means doing your teaching job professionally and with care. Finally, it means being fair and consistent in your treatment of each student. If teachers just enforce discipline and insist on inmate orderliness, they risk triggering conflict and an undesirable evaluation as being 'rigid' or 'punitive' for such enforcement interferes with the individualised treatment students need.

Theme 2: *Respect as personal relationship*

The second theme that weaves through the interview with Anne is that respect involves a personal relationship, where people are concerned to communicate, to achieve mutual understanding, to demonstrate concern for others. Respect is not something that exists in abstraction, it exists in relationships. Whereas John, the prison officer, saw individual relationships with prisoners as undesirable and problematic, Anne's impression is that young offenders come to respect and appreciate officers with whom they have personal and sustained interactions.

Theme 3: *Prisoners' respect as sameness and conformity*

The last theme identified in Anne's interview has to do with some of the requisites deemed necessary for gaining respect from the young offenders' point of view. Anne believes that young offenders may be forced into behaving in certain ways or into taking some actions by virtue of compelling forces they encounter within the YOI and in society at large. Anne recounts an episode in which one of her students failed an exam on purpose because he feared the repercussions should he pass:

> *I know one kid who failed his exam purposely he told this other teacher 'oh I failed on purpose so I'd look good' and so he gets respect.*

Anne's discourse of respect

Anne's talk emphasising relationships, mutual understanding and concern suggests a discourse of care based on the conviction that it is necessary to address her students' needs and manage their learning environment through responsibility, competence and sensitivity to the particular social and physical environment in which instruction is taking place. Anne frequently refers to the young offenders as 'kids', a word choice that certainly makes the prisoners less threatening by reminding us of their young age and suggests that she is aware of these young people's transition status between childhood and adulthood.

Respect as your first move: Barbara, a Library Assistant

Barbara is in her mid-50s, works as a Library Assistant in the Education Wing Library, and has a long experience of working with disadvantaged youth in community centres.

Theme 1: *Respect as appreciation of the worth of the other*

The first theme that arose from this interview is respect as appreciation of the worth of the other. This appreciation can be linked to a recognition of the other's value because of their merits, abilities and achievements, as in the case of teachers who are respected by young offenders because they are able to deliver their subject matter in an interesting and stimulating way. However, for Barbara, recognising the worth of the other seems to be an *a priori* principle, that is, she believes that recognition of the worth of other people is not based on an evaluation of their quality and value, or on our experiences with these persons, but is somehow independent of them and prior to it. As an *a priori* stance, respect is granted by Barbara to young offenders immediately, at her first encounter with them, as in the following episode where she is to make a decision about how to call prisoners:

> *when I started I wanted to know their first names because everyone calls them by their surnames and with one of them today I interspersed between his first name and his surname and then I realized I'm calling him Mr which I found quite respectful.*

Theme 2: *Respect involves sensitivity and consideration of the other*

The second theme that emerged from the data is that if you respect someone you deal sensitively and empathically with them. Barbara remembers an episode when she chose to deal with one of the offenders in a way that would not create hurt feelings or damage his pride:

> *I had to tell one off the other day I didn't ball that out in the library I took him into the office spoke to him there.*

Barbara believes that young offenders can learn from mistakes if they are handled in a sensitive way and are accompanied by a broader, more important recognition of their experiences of success. Barbara regrets that the officers do not show enough consideration and understanding for the offenders at times:

> *one of them had to be taken for mandate drugs test I thought the officer was a bit off hand because he was being taken away in front of everybody and I wasn't happy with that.*

Barbara's discourse of respect

The analysis of Barbara's interview reveals a discourse of sensitivity, empathy, and consideration, alongside a discourse of understanding the experiential features of imprisonment and prisoners as individuals. For Barbara, respect is not only possible to gain in prison, but is the natural and obvious way to behave when dealing with young offenders, and she is not afraid of coming across as weak and vulnerable if she admits that she is wrong or praises an offender for what he has done: "*in the YOI if somebody has done something really good I would say thank you for doing that*".

Respect as consistency: Martin, an Entry Level Maths teacher

Martin is in his mid-50s, and taught science for nearly 30 years in comprehensive schools before teaching in HMYOIX.
Theme 1: *Consistent behaviour on the part of the teachers fosters an environment of respect*

The first theme that arises from this interview is that of consistency, with Martin claiming that an environment of respect is fostered by consistent behaviour on the part of teachers and management. Martin develops this theme further through a discussion of the impact of the inconsistent behaviour of some teachers on classroom discipline and the wider environment of respect in the Education Wing. Non-enforcement of rules leads to an environment of disrespect because some teachers have to make up for the behaviour of other teachers by being overly strict and authoritative, leading to conflict in the classroom.

Foucault (1977) introduced the concept of 'infra-penalty' to refer to the power of correctional staff and administrators to judge on the conduct of prisoners within custodial institutions. When inmates' conduct violates institutional rules or is simply perceived as 'out of line', custodial staff may enforce punitive measures that involve warnings, negative reports, deprivations and petty humiliations. Martin mentions one of the measures used by teachers to enforce discipline, the IEP[5] reports. He questions, however, their validity to ensure a climate of respect in classrooms:

> *in your lesson if a student is misbehaving then you give 'em a negative IEP but the offenders will argue the case with you so a system that's supposed you saying we won't have disruption within the lesson actually becomes an arguing point.*

What Martin ultimately believes in thus seems to be not a system of even stricter disciplinary measures but having a coherent system of values and attitudes that will influence the relationship between teachers and offenders and the latter's behaviour.

Theme 2: *Respect as a relationship built on values and boundaries*

Martin believes in the power of establishing positive relationships with prisoners built on values and recognition of boundaries that define the specific educational environment. He identifies some of the fundamental values that must underpin the ethos and the practice of the institution by way of consistency, professional competence, skills and conduct. The right way to progress in order to create a relationship of respect is to behave consistently by committing to an ethical standard of practice that recognises the boundaries in teacher/prisoner interactions and the boundaries in classroom behaviour.

Martin believes that restorative justice can only work if the overall environment is one of accountability, responsibility and values. There is

---

[5] IEP (Incentive and Earned Privilege) is a system of evaluation of a prisoner's status that includes three levels: basic, standard and enhanced. Each level deals with various privileges being awarded.

no point in trying to introduce restorative justice practices in prison if what offenders see around them conflicts with what they are told to believe in.

Martin's discourse of respect

Martin's discourse revolves around the concept of consistency, a mantra that runs throughout the interview. Martin seems to interpret consistency either as predictability, establishing and ensuring the same standard of practices and behaviour across the institution, or as reliability of teachers and staff to work and behave honestly, ethically and with integrity. Consistency is a primary factor for respect. A lack of consistency in teaching and discipline strategies across the Education Department is the cause of the lack of respect he observes in the institution. Insistence upon consistency seems to betray an authoritative discourse where little voice is left to the young offenders. There is little space for discussion in Martin's discourse of classroom practice and his discourse emerges as primarily monologic. He does not report on particular episodes involving the young offenders themselves. His interest seems focused primarily on the teachers, managers and officers as active subjects in the Education Department, with the offenders left as the passive subjects on whom teaching is bestowed.

Foucault (1977) noticed that authoritarian discourses become powerful when they are sanctioned by and indissolubly fused with institutions. In prisons one of the prevailing discourses is that of control, together with those of rehabilitation and normalisation. The discourse of control refers to complete order and predictability determined by rigid rules aimed at establishing a smooth management of the establishment (Welch 2009). Martin's notion of consistency insists on predictable repetitions of patterns, and therefore bears the features of a discourse of control.

Discussion and Conclusion

The aim of this research was to identify and describe the discourses of respect that inform and shape prisoner–staff communications and interactions in a young offenders institution. As mentioned in the introductory section, previous research on respect in prisons has highlighted some of the difficulties and challenges experienced by prison staff in establishing and maintaining respectful relationships with prisoners, and has pointed to the prevalence in prisons of disciplinary discourses of respect as obedience and deference to authority. While confirming the existence of authoritarian discourses of respect in a young offenders institution, the data analysed in this study also provide evidence of a range of other discourses through which staff working with young prisoners experience and construct their understanding of respect and their social practices. Authoritarian discourses were employed not only by prison uniformed staff, as hypothesised at the start of the research, but also by one of the teachers who identified in consistency, predictability and control some of the core features of respect.

One of the most important conclusions of this research is that respect is not something that exists in abstraction; rather, it exists in social interaction and in relationships, where each of the parties is ready and willing to acknowledge the other's individuality and worth. This aspect of respect fits well into the general context of restorative justice principles and practices. Leading restorative justice theorists such as Zehr (1990), Braithwaite (2002), Van Ness / Strong (2006), Edgar / Newell (2006) and Liebmann (2007), claim that misbehaviour should be understood as a violation of people and relationships, thus stressing the personal nature of restorative justice in contrast with the impersonal nature of the retributive justice system. Reparation of the personal consequences of misbehaviour is achieved through the development of personal relationships that aim not only at repairing the harm done but also at reducing anti-social behaviour and creating community cohesion. As we saw above, respect has emerged in this research as an essential ingredient in personal relationships. All teachers and civilian staff participating in this research acknowledge the relevance of respect in ensuring positive and constructive interpersonal relationships.

Research on the relevance of interpersonal relationships in custodial establishments (Wortley 2002, Harvey 2007, Crewe 2009) has investigated the mechanisms underlying prisoner-staff violence in custodial establishments. Most assaults on staff tend to occur during ordinary interactions with offenders and the quality of interpersonal relationships with prisoners is a significant determinant in assessing the likelihood of attacks. The nature of relationships and how interactions are conducted have emerged as having a significant bearing on prisoner-staff violence. The findings of the present study confirm the need for attention to relationships and relationship building in conducting restorative meetings for incidents between staff and offenders.

In promoting restorative practices of conflict resolution in such a hierarchical and authoritarian structure as a prison, it is worth considering the point made by Miller (2001) and De Cremer / Tyler (2005) that the kind of respect required from in-group members is different from that demanded from out-group members. In the context researched in this study, a prison for young men aged 18-21, where there are strong peer affiliations, bonds and influences this means that some features of the interactional respect among young offenders are likely to diverge from those of respect between offenders and prison staff. What can be felt as highly disrespectful in an interchange with officers and other prison staff may be perceived as completely innocuous in the occurrence of an in-group interaction, and vice versa. Linked to the above, another important factor to be taken into account in evaluating interactional respect is the power relationship existing between the parties. The features of respect demanded from someone perceived as lower-status will differ from those required from someone considered higher-status. The different nature of respect in dependence of the power relationship among the parties has a vital bearing upon restorative meetings, where people often belonging to completely different age, social and cultural groups are brought together and asked to develop a relationship of mutual respect.

In conclusion, this study has provided important insights into the components and dynamics of respect within an educational custodial setting and into some of the issues and questions that need to be addressed in promoting the use of restorative justice in prisons. It is hoped that these findings will assist teachers and practitioners involved in restorative justice intervention and will serve as a starting point for further research on this topic.

References

Bakhtin, Mikhail 1981. *The Dialogic Imagination*. Trans. C. Emerson and M.Holquist. Austin: University of Texas Press.

Braithwaite, John 2002. *Restorative Justice and Responsive Regulation*. Oxford: Oxford University Press.

Butler, Michelle / Drake, Deborah 2007. Reconsidering respect: its role in Her Majesty's Prison Service. *The Howard Journal of Criminal Justice* 46(2): 115-127.

Butler, Michelle 2008. What are you looking at? Prisoner confrontations and the search for respect. *The British Journal of Criminology* 48(6): 856-873.

Crewe, Ben 2009. *The Prisoner Society: Power, Adaptation, and Social Life in an English Prison*. Oxford: Oxford University Press.

De Cremer, David / Tyler, Tom 2005. Am I respected or not? Inclusion and reputation as issues in group membership. *Social Justice Research* 18(2): 121-153.

Edgar, Kimmet / Newell, Tim 2006. *Restorative Justice in Prisons. A guide to making it happen*. Winchester: Waterside Press.

Foucault, Michael 1977. *Discipline and Punish: The Birth of the Prison*. Trans. A. Sheridan. New York: Vintage.

—. 1980. Body/Power. In *Power / Knowledge: Selected Interviews and Other Writings, 1972-1977*. Trans. C. Gordon. Brighton: Harvester Press: 55-62.

Harvey, Joel 2007. *Young Men in Prison: Surviving and Adapting to Life Inside*. Cullompton: Willan.

Hornsey, Matthew / Jetten, Jolanda 2004. The individual within the group: balancing the need to belong with the need to be different. *Personality and Social Psychology Review* 8(3): 248-264.

Jenkins, David 1991. Respect in prison. In *Respect in Prison. The Transcript of a Conference held 11th–14th July 1991 at Bishop Grossteste College, Lincoln*. Lincoln: The Bishop's House.

Krimsky, Sheldon / Simoncelli, Tania 2011. *Genetic Justice: DNA Data Banks, Criminal Investigations, and Civil Liberties*. New York: Columbia University Press.

Liebling, Alison (assisted by Helen Arnold) 2004. *Prisons and their Moral Performance: A Study of Values, Quality and Prison Life*. Oxford: Oxford University Press.

Liebmann, Marian 2007. *Restorative Justice. How it works*. London and Philadelphia: Jessica Kingsley.

Miller, Dale 2001. Disrespect and the experience of injustice. *Annual Review of Psychology* 52: 527-553.

Van Ness, Daniel / Strong, Karen 2006. *Restoring Justice* (3rd ed.). Cincinnati: Anderson.

Welch, Michael 2009. *Crimes of Power and States of Impunity: The US Response to Terror*. New Brunswick, N.J.: Rutgers University Press.

Wortley, Richard 2002. *Situational Prison Control: Crime Prevention in Correctional Institutions*. Cambridge: Cambridge University Press.

Zehr, Howard 1990. *Changing Lenses: A New Focus for Crime and Justice*. Scottsdale, PA: Herald Press.

CHAPTER SIX

CONSTRUCTING AUTHORITY IN INTERNATIONAL INVESTMENT ARBITRATION: INSIGHTS FROM SEPARATE OPINIONS AT ICSID

RUTH BREEZE

Introduction

Some critical attention has recently focused on arbitration practices across the world, with a view to determining whether arbitration genuinely provides an alternative to litigation, or whether it is being colonised by practices more typical in a context of litigation (Bhatia et al. 2008). Much of this work deals with areas such as commercial arbitration, however, and less attention has been paid to the type of international investment arbitration carried out in institutions such as the International Centre for the Settlement of Investment Disputes (ICSID). In principle, investment disputes should be resolved in terms of the relevant Bilateral Investment Treaties and the pertinent arbitration rules in order to provide a fair decision in a particular case, and the decision makers are in no sense bound by precedent as would be the case in a common law court. Yet there is growing evidence that a body of case law is developing within ICSID itself, and that arbitrators are increasingly referring to previous awards as precedents. This issue is controversial within the arbitration community, since some commentators see it as a departure from the principles and methods of arbitration, or possibly even as an invasion of practices habitual in common law systems. One problem when researching this topic is that most ICSID proceedings are confidential, and only the final award is published. It is thus difficult to ascertain what principles or authorities have shaped the arbitrators' thinking about the issues under discussion. One source of information about arbitral proceedings which is rarely consulted, but which sheds considerable light on current practices, is the separate opinion. These dissenting or concurring opinions may be published alongside the award if an arbitrator wishes to take issue with some point of the majority decision, and they provide evidence of the arguments and sources that were brought to bear during the analysis of the case.

This chapter provides an in-depth study of the sources referred to in the 14 available dissenting opinions published by ICSID on its website between 1990 and 2008. It considers the evidence as to what sources are used, and analyses the different types of other-reference found (Hyland 1999; Ädel / Garrettson 2006). The findings are illuminated by argumentation analysis (White 2003: 265-275) to distinguish what role these references play in the text, and to what extent these sources are simply entertained, or how far they are applied authoritatively to produce dialogic contraction and resolve the issues at stake. The study reveals a specific range of sources to which arbitrators appeal, and adds further evidence that previous ICSID decisions are increasingly being understood to constitute a body of case law to be applied to future cases.

Background

The practice of issuing dissenting or concurring opinions is thought to have originated in the House of Lords, where each Law Lord declared his/her opinion separately and could offer a different point of view (Hussain 1984). Such opinions are allowed by the court systems of many countries with a Common Law tradition, including the United States. In the context of international disputes, dissenting opinions have been an object of controversy since early times, since the publication of separate opinions is felt by some critics to undermine stakeholders' confidence in the decision. Most of the arbitration rules currently in force are silent on this matter: separate opinions are neither encouraged nor prohibited by the International Chamber of Commerce (ICC), the London Court of International Arbitration (LCIA), the World Intellectual Property Organization (WIPO) or the United Nations Commission on International Trade Law (UNCITRAL) arbitral rules. However, the Iran-US Claims Tribunal, operating under UNCITRAL rules, expressly adds instructions about dissenting opinions, and frequently produces them. It seems likely that the use of such opinions by this influential Tribunal has made this practice more widespread (Sanders 1999: 284). The ICSID Convention (ICSID 2006) expressly permits separate opinions: Article 48 (4) states:

"Any member of the Tribunal may attach his individual opinion to the Award, whether he dissents from the majority or not, or a statement of his dissent".

In the present case, since ICSID sessions are held behind closed doors and only the award is published, separate opinions provide valuable insights into the way arbitral decisions are made. Examination of these opinions will afford us a deeper understanding of arbitration processes and discourses. Elsewhere, the present author has discussed reasons for dissent and analysed the pragmatic strategies used to present divergent opinions in a persuasive way (Breeze 2012a; Breeze 2012b). This chapter focuses on how arbitrators refer to sources and principles outside the immediate context of the case to provide a solid basis for their argumentation. It aims to determine how, other than by reasoning alone, arbitrators bolster their own arguments by appealing to authoritative sources. This is of crucial importance, because arbitration is generally understood to provide a balanced, objective and neutral means of resolving disputes which is not tied to the legal system or tradition of a particular country. In particular, the creators of arbitral systems did not envisage the establishment of a new quasi-judicial system of precedent mirroring what is found in common law systems (Brunet 1992; Scheuer 2001; Commission 2007; Wangelin 2004; Bhatia et al. 2008). Nonetheless, there is some recent evidence that in their search to ground their arguments, arbitrators reach out with increasing frequency to other sources, and in particular to previous arbitral decisions that are held to encapsulate particular principles or provide something akin to a precedent that can be used to resolve the case at hand (Weidemeyer 2010).

In what follows, we address the question as to what sources ICSID arbitrators refer to, and how these references are formulated. We shall use elements of reference analysis (Ädel / Garrettson 2006) to examine how these sources are presented, and heteroglossic engagement analysis (White 2003) to see how far the sources or principles quoted are used to "open up" the argument to different views, or how far they "close down" the argument in a way that is intended to be definitive.

Reference to sources in separate opinions

Before analysing the 14 separate opinions, it is useful to consider what kinds of sources would generally be regarded as pertinent in ICSID arbitration. In ICSID cases we might expect arbitrators to call on international agreements such as the ICSID convention itself, or the ICSID rules which govern arbitration proceedings. Since ICSID cases involve investment treaties between states, it would also be quite usual for the Bilateral Investment Treaty in question to be called upon, as well as broader trade agreements such as the North American Free Trade Agreement (NAFTA).

Nonetheless, a cursory reading of the 14 opinions in the present sample reveals a much wider range of sources used by these arbitrators to ground their arguments and lend credence to their opinions. These include the following: previous ICSID awards; previous non-ICSID awards; academic papers or reference works; and general principles or adages.

Academic papers or works of reference

Most of the academic sources cited in these opinions are reference works such as commentaries and textbooks: commentaries on the ICSID convention, on previous ICSID cases, expert commentaries on NAFTA, on the Iran-US Claims Tribunal, and on cases at the International Court of Justice and the Permanent Court of International Justice. Use of such sources appears to be more a matter of personal style than of general professional practice, since some arbitrators make copious use of these sources, whereas others do not refer to them at all.

Two of the arbitrators in particular make fairly substantial reference to academic sources, particularly to authoritative works concerning the law of treaties, and to books on the principles of public international law.

> Czar: La doctrina jurídica ha desarrollado multiplicidad de teorías y producido infinidad de escritos al respecto. Siguiendo a Fitzmaurice es aconsejable reconocer […] Ian Sinclair nos recuerda que […]
>
> Rovine: For an important article calling for caution, see Caron […] Todd Weiler writes in the generally accepted way that […] One scholar put it this way […]

In these references, both give prominence to the authors, generally mentioning his/her name first, then using a speech act verb to connect the author to the idea or statement. However, it is noticeable that in the first case, these references are offered in a more discursive, conciliatory tone, as though they formed part of an academic discussion rather than an arbitral opinion. The language accordingly offers more features of expansion, including acknowledgement of different possible viewpoints: in this example, we should particularly note Czar's recognition of "multiple" theories and "infinite" writings on the subject at hand, which would seem to open up a wealth of possibilities rather than narrowing down the scope. It should perhaps also be noted that the Argentinian arbitrator's concept of "doctrina jurídica" may merge case law with academic commentaries in a very broad concept of jurisprudence characteristic of Spanish-based legal systems. Czar's use of these references appears to be to establish dialogue with the ideas they contain, rather than to reinforce a particular argument. In contrast to this, Rovine's comments offer less openness, tending to dialogic contraction by stressing the "normative" and "important" nature of what these academic writers have to say. Rather than opening up a discussion of the issues, Rovine is using academic references to work towards a definitive argument.

Previous ICSID awards

It is striking that these arbitrators often make reference to previous ICSID awards. After all, there is no doctrine of *stare decisis* in arbitration, and much arbitration literature claims that arbitration simply does not create precedent (Brunet 1992; Commission 2007). The ICSID was certainly not designed to generate a system of precedent running parallel to that of national common law systems. However, there is some evidence to suggest that ICSID tribunals have gradually built up what has been called an "investment treaty case law or jurisprudence" (Weidemeyer 2010). The trend detected here is fully consistent with a recent study of ICSID awards and decisions, which shows that there is an increasing tendency for arbitrators to cite previous ICSID cases in their arguments (Weidemeyer 2010). Up until 1994, the highest number of prior ICSID decisions or awards that had been cited in any ICSID decision or award was two. However, these authors found that the mean number of previous cases cited per award or decision has increased rapidly in the last few years: in 2002, each award cited a mean of 3 previous cases, while by 2004 this figure had risen to 4.5, and in 2006 each award mentioned a mean of 9.3 previous ICSID cases. The same trend can be observed in the separate opinions examined in the present study.

Table 6-1 shows that the trend towards referring to previous ICSID cases in separate opinions has been gathering momentum over the last 20 years. It should be noted that the table indicates only the number of cases referred to, rather than the number of times such cases were mentioned.

Year	Total number of separate opinions	Total number of previous ICSID cases cited
1990	1	0
2000	1	3
2002	2	0
2004	1	4
2007	6	9
2008	3	10

Table 6-1 Number of previous ICSID cases cited per year in separate opinions

In these opinions, most arbitrators seem to refer to previous ICSID cases as a matter of course, in the tacit assumption that previous decisions constitute a logical, accepted basis for making the present decision:

> Berman: The award clearly fails to meet the accepted requirement (as enunciated in the Annulment Decision in MINE v. Guinea) that "the requirement that an award has to be motivated implies that it must enable the reader to follow the reasoning of the Tribunal on points of fact and law".
>
> Highet: Here, reference may be made to the recent award in the *Azinian* case referred to by Respondent.

Moreover, this tendency is not confined to opinions by arbitrators from a common law background:

> Czar: El Tribunal, apoyándose en abundantes antecedentes CIADI, afirmó: "In performing this task, the Tribunal will apply a prima facie standard, both to the determination of the meaning and scope of the BIT provisions and to the assessment whether the facts alleged may constitute breaches.
>
> Witt: Il a été defini, d'une manière que fait autorité, *comme étant "un désaccord sur un point de droit ou de fait, une contradiction, une opposition de thèses juridiques ou d'intérêts entre deux personnes"* (the reference is to the influential ICSID case ARB/03/4 often referred to as "Luchetti").

Even taking into account the different resonance of terms such as *autorité* and *antecedente* in the languages in question, these examples suggest that a similar process of appeal to precedent is at work in the opinions by Czar and Witt as in the other opinions.

Arbitrators also make explicit reference to the importance of the award under discussion in setting a precedent for future ICSID decisions and other investment treaty disputes:

> Highet: The precedential significance of this Award for future proceedings under the North American Free Trade Agreement (NAFTA) cannot be underestimated.

Notably, the opinions in this sample also contain evidence that the use of precedent is often contested in arbitral proceedings. The following examples serve as evidence that these arbitrators, at least, are willing to take issue with their counterparts' use of "precedent", or even to reject decisions made in previous cases:

> Lowenfeld: The majority feels the need to defend its conclusion with more irrelevant discussion of the *Loewen* case, the Vienna Convention of the Law of Treaties, and unrelated cases.

> Berman: No authority is given for this proposition arising out of the BIT itself; the only authority is a very old decision of the Permanent Court of International Justice (and a recent ICSID Award which the ad hoc Committee rightly finds to be out of context…).

All of this serves as evidence that the tendency to regard ICSID awards as creating precedent is gathering momentum. The vast majority of references to earlier ICSID awards is phrased in such a way that the earlier award is taken as a touchstone of rightness. However, arbitrators also resist it, insisting on the need to reject inappropriate applications of arbitral "precedent", and their right to make fresh decisions without being bound by previous rulings as might be the case in Common Law judicial systems.

Previous non-ICSID awards

It is also relatively frequent for the separate opinions in this sample to cite awards and decisions from other courts or arbitration panels. However, the trend documented above towards greater citation of ICSID awards as precedents seems to be counterbalanced by a tendency to cite the decisions of other tribunals less as time goes by. In concrete terms, the four opinions published between 1990 and 2002 make reference to International Court of Justice/Permanent International Court of Justice (ICJ/PICJ) decisions (9 citations), while also quoting decisions from UNCITRAL arbitration, the Iran-US Claims Commission, and from much earlier sources such as the Italy-Venezuela Mixed Claims Commission, the Mexico-America Commission, or the America-Venezuela Claims Commission. By contrast, the ten opinions published in the period 2004-2008 make reference to the ICJ/PICJ (5 times), and to the Iran-US Claims Commission (4 times), as well as once to an UNCITRAL award.

Regarding the manner of citation, however, there appears to be little difference in the weight given to antecedents from one court or another, as arbitrators seem to refer indiscriminately to decisions from ICSID and other arbitral tribunals:

> Born: That is clearly recognized in prior authority in this context (referring to two previous ICSID awards and one UNCITRAL award).

> Berman: No authority is given for this proposition arising out of the BIT itself; the only authority is a very old decision of the Permanent Court of International Justice (and a recent ICSID Award ...).

On one level, the trend towards citing previous ICSID decisions more, and other arbitral tribunals less, would seem to be explicable in terms of practicality and availability. International investment disputes tend to revolve around a specific, relatively limited, set of issues, and it is logical to seek solutions in the way earlier arbitrators have handled similar cases in the past. When ICSID arbitration was first introduced, it was not possible to refer to ICSID precedents, because none existed. Arbitrators therefore reached out to examples from similar institutions across the world in order to find patterns that would help to reach a decision or principles that would underpin their argumentation. Now that ICSID arbitration is better established, with abundant published awards and decisions on the institutional webpage, and weighty volumes of commentary by distinguished experts, it is becoming increasingly usual to cite prior ICSID cases as precedents.

General principles and adages

The arbitrators in this sample also often draw upon "general principles", sometimes expressed in the form of Latin adages:

> Born: It is ancient law that there is no right without a remedy (ubi jus ibi remedium) and that adage applies here no less than elsewhere.

> Covarrubias: It is a general principle of law that the burden of proof lies with the party who alleges the affirmative of any proposition: necessitas probandi incumbit illi qui agit.

As is often the case with maxims in other contexts, the pragmatic function of these is to lend force to the statement, convert what might otherwise seem to be a mere argument into an incontrovertible truth. An adage or saying is authoritative merely by virtue of being one, it seems: it is interesting that most of the adages are fronted by a description such as "the principle that" or "the old adage that". This effect is heightened by the arbitrators' use of adjectives such as "customary", "well-settled", "general", "elementary", in order to increase the standing of the principle quoted.

Analytical approaches

Referencing systems

The pragmatics of reference to previous writers has been studied in some depth in the field of academic English. Swales (1990), Hyland (1999) and Ädel / Garretson (2006) have conducted detailed analyses of reference to prior research in academic writing, understanding referencing as a broad category which includes examples such as those in 1, 2 and 3 below (from Ädel / Garretson 2006: 272):

1. It is the individual's given expressions that define the basis for how the group will interact with the individual (Goffman, 1960).

2. *Bourdieu argues that* the subjective moment is crucial in constructing class since "agents are both classified and classifiers" (Bourdieu 1987: 5).

3. *Durkheim's theory* is very attractive.

Ädel / Garretson develop a threefold system for analysing references, which distinguishes between "citation", "attribution" and "mention". Citation is a reference to a source when the writer or work is not integrated into the text, corresponding to what Swales calls "non-integral reference" (1990). Attribution is when some linguistic or cognitive act is attributed to a source in a syntactically integrated manner, corresponding to what other writers term "integral reference" (Swales 1990; Hyland 1999). Ädel and Garretson's third term, "mention", covers all the cases in which a writer simply refers to an author or one of his/her ideas or publications without attributing any particular statement to him/her. Thus example 1 above illustrates citation, example 2 shows attribution, in which a speech act verb is used to attribute the idea to the author, and example 3, mention, in which a source is mentioned, but his/her/its words are not reported.

In the separate opinions, all three types of reference are used: the three examples below again illustrate citation (1), attribution (2) and mention (3). It should be noted that citation tends to foreground the idea, which is integrated into the arbitrator's own discourse and for which he/she takes responsibility. Attribution, on the other hand, seems to foreground the source: the arbitrator both offloads some of the responsibility for what is said onto the source, so that it is not framed entirely as his/her own opinion, and at the same time lends greater importance to what is said, because of the authoritative nature of the source. Mention, which is rare in this sample, is not generally used in the main lines of argument:

> 1. Weil: The latter type of dispute is to be settled by domestic procedures, notably before domestic courts. (footnote to Schreuer, C. The ICSID Convention: A Commentary)
>
> 2. Asante: I am fortified in this view by the authoritative account of the evolution of the British bilateral investment treaties by Denza and Brooks [...] who explained the relationship between customary international law and the provisions of the UK bilateral investment treaties as follows: "Careful thought was given as to [...]"
>
> 3. Weil: This does not mean that I would be inclined to ignore or put into question the flexible approach adopted in previous ICSID cases—in particular the *Holiday Inns v. Morocco* and *Fedax v. Venezuela* cases.

	ICSID cases	**Non-ICSID arbitration cases**	**Academic sources**
1. Cite	8	3	11
2. Attribute	28	35	38
3. Mention	19	11	2

Table 6-2 Types of reference used to refer to ICSID cases, non-ICSID cases and academic sources

As Table 6-2 shows, by far the most frequent way of referring to sources here is assertion, in which a writer or tribunal is represented as the direct "speaker". Consider the following two examples:

> Highet: In that Award (Azinian), the Tribunal stated most precisely that "A governmental authority surely cannot be faulted for acting in a manner

> validated by its courts unless the courts themselves are disavowed at an international level".
>
> Weil: As Professor Schreuer writes, the basic idea of the Convention, as expressed in its title, is to provide for dispute settlement between States and foreign investors.

In both cases, the source is named and placed before the idea attributed to it, which is given either as a direct quotation or as a paraphrase. A reporting verb ("stated", "writes") is used to attribute the idea to its originator. In both cases, the use of this structure gives prominence to the source. The source is of great importance in the arbitrator's argument, because it lends credibility to the idea that is expressed. It is logical to assume that the dissenting arbitrators' preference for attribution is related to their need to add force to their own arguments by quoting established authorities or influential previous decisions. Their use of the source as reinforcement is often strengthened by the use of reporting verbs denoting certainty, such as "states", "specifies", "indicates", "held" and "declared". On some occasions, further emphasis is added: "expressly states", "expressly rejected"; "is lucidly stated", "rightly points out".

If we compare these findings with those described by Hyland (1999) for academic writing, we can observe that reference plays quite a different role in these arbitral opinions. The overall purpose of citation in academic writing is to allow writers to "establish a persuasive epistemological and social framework for the acceptance of their arguments" (1999: 344). The way this is put into practice varies from one discourse community to another. In the humanities, writers build up a context by quoting previous work, and use sources to negotiate their way through a complex network of ideas, while scientists are more likely to downplay human agency and foreground findings and ideas. In the case of ICSID opinions, the use of citation is quite different: here, the arbitrators are not so much concerned with acknowledging "the role of individuals in creating knowledge" (Hyland 1999: 355), as using authoritative figures and previous arbitral decisions to underpin and strengthen their own arguments. By naming experts and quoting important awards, they build up their own arguments on what is understood to be a solid basis, much in the way that a common law lawyer would build up an argument on precedent.

Endorsement and dialogic contraction

It is generally understood that all utterances in some sense take into account or respond to prior utterances, and, to some degree, anticipate or acknowledge likely responses, reactions and objections from actual or potential dialogic partners (White 2003). When presenting an argument, the speaker/writer can open up the dialogue to divergent positions, or close it down, moving towards a definitive position. One resource that writers can use is termed "extravocalisation" (Martin / White 2004), that is, the inclusion in the text of an explicitly external voice. The rhetorical effect of quoting others is often similar to that of a "pronouncement", in which a writer interpolates him/herself directly into the text, but with the difference that some degree of responsibility for what is quoted is offloaded onto the source, rather than assumed by the writer. As White points out (2012), the degree of arguability that the writer allows is rather limited as a consequence of the high expertise associated with the source. If the source is highly authoritative, little scope is left to negotiate alternative positions. By aligning him/herself with an authoritative source, the writer is both claiming authority and offloading responsibility.

In the present sample, use of verbs like "specify" and "declare" when reporting previous arbitral cases, for example, indicates that the author fully endorses what the source says. In this case, the use of non-hedged verbs of assertion brings these utterances close to what Martin and White (2004) term "proclamation", which is often used in an argument to advance a viewpoint against some possible alternative position which may not be made explicit. It is clear that the writer is using a high-status, high-authority source and fully endorsing that source. The writer is thereby constructing an authoritative textual persona for him/herself. But this is being done in a context of official dissent against a majority decision, and is therefore dialogic. In almost all the cases examined here, the invocation of sources in these opinions (reference to academic works, awards, adages) is used as a resource of dialogic contraction. The arbitrators almost always indicate tacit or explicit agreement with the author or decision quoted, which they are using to argue against a majority decision that may or may not be outlined in the text. Previous ICSID decisions, other arbitral awards, academic texts or adages are applied to fend off or restrict the scope of alternative positions. Writers stress the "normative" and "important" nature of what they are quoting – they reinforce the quotations and the quotations reinforce them. These are discourse-contracting references, designed to bolster the writer's own line of argumentation.

Examination of the evidence in this sample seems to suggest that arbitrators use their sources carefully to build up the force of their argument. In this, although the reasoning itself is of great importance, the identity and nature of the source appear to play a significant role in adding credibility and weight to the arguments. The name of the source is given a prominent position before the idea that is attributed to it, and the sense of certainty and reliability is emphasised by the use of uncompromising speech act verbs and emphatic adverbs when quoting or summarising words or ideas from the source.

Conclusions

Let us briefly consider the nature of the sources referred to in these opinions, and then move on to the ways that they are quoted. Of all the types of source referred to as providing authority here, those which are framed as constituting precedent are potentially the most controversial. It is logical that arbitrators should reach for general principles expressed in legal adages, or should call on commentaries on the ICSID convention. However, the tendency to use previous cases as precedent, much as common law counsel would, has given rise to greater polemic.

Various explanations have been put forward concerning the growing tendency to cite previous ICSID awards as "precedent". It has been argued that this trend is encouraged by the presence of published, reasoned Awards (Commission 2007). It is also thought to be fuelled by the desire to give "equal treatment" to all cases (Weidemeyer 2010) since when there is a problem with a state, a large number of similarly situated investors may assert claims under the particular treaty or one like it. Where many similar cases are going to arise, it makes sense to follow similar principles when resolving them. A consistent approach may help to legitimise ICSID in the eyes of its critics, making it appear more reliable and transparent (Commission 2007). There is also some evidence that precedent serves as a "gap filler" in cases where there is no clear answer to the problems raised, although questions concerning the value of past awards are likely to be hotly contested (Weidemeyer 2010). We may also surmise that the use of precedent is an overflow of habits from one area of professional life to another. Most arbitrators are barristers with a background in common law practice. When faced with the need to resolve a problem, they are likely to reach out for the tools that have served them well in other areas of their professional life.

Nevertheless, some feel that the general move towards creation of precedent in ICSID arbitration may be felt to run counter to its basic principles, namely to provide ad hoc solutions to particular problems (Gélinas 2005; Weidemeyer 2010). Most particularly, there may be a problem because the role that precedent has come to play in investment treaty arbitration today increasingly resembles the common law doctrine of *stare decisis* – but notably without the associated values and compensatory mechanisms that inform common law systems (Commission 2007).

The evidence we have considered here, concerning the kind of sources to which arbitrators refer, suggests that a growing body of what might be called arbitral case law is coming into use in the resolution of investment disputes. Earlier opinions reach out to awards from other institutions, while more recent ones refer more to awards from ICSID itself. The discoursal study of the way in which these sources are presented in the text confirms that they are being used to add credibility and weight to the arguments, boosting the authority of the writer. The referencing pattern favouring assertion to accord a prominent position to the source, and the use of categorical *verba dicendi*, mean that such references generally have the effect of closing down dialogue and moving towards a definitive position. In short, the discourse study indicates that previous arbitral decisions are being used in these arguments much in the way that precedents would be used in common law pleadings or judgments.

References

Ädel, Annelie / Garretson, Gregory 2006. Citation practices across the disciplines: the case of proficient student writing. In Pérez-Llantada Auría, M. C. / Pló Alastrué R. / Neumann C. P. (eds.) *Academic and Professional Communication in the 21st Century: Genres, Rhetoric and the Construction of Disciplinary Knowledge. Proceedings of the 5th International AELFE Conference*. Zaragoza: Prensas Universitarias de Zaragoza: 271-280.

Bhatia, Vijay K. / Candlin, Christopher N. / Engberg, Jan 2008. Concepts, contexts and procedures in arbitration discourse. In Bhatia, V. K. / Candlin, C. / Engberg, J. (eds.) *Legal Discourse across Cultures and Systems*. Hong Kong: Hong Kong University Press: 127-144.

Breeze, Ruth 2012a. Dissenting and concurring opinions in international investment arbitration: how the arbitrators frame their need to differ. *International Journal for the Semiotics of Law* 25(3): 1-21.

—. 2012b. With the greatest respect for my colleagues. Politeness in dissenting opinions in international arbitration disputes. In Padilla Cruz M. / Fernández Amaya L. (eds.) *New Perspectives on (Im)Politeness and Interpersonal* Communication. Newcastle: Cambridge Scholars Press: 220-237.

Brunet, Edward J. 1992. Arbitration and constitutional rights. *North Carolina Law Review* 71: 81-120.

Commission, Jeffery P. 2007. Precedent in investment treaty arbitration: a citation analysis of a developing jurisprudence. *Journal of International Arbitration* 24: 149–150.

Gélinas, Fabien. 2005. Investment tribunals and the commercial arbitration model: Mixed procedures and creeping institutionalisation. In Gehring M. W. / Cordonier Segger, M. C. (eds.) *Sustainable Developments in World Trade Law*. The Hague: Kluwer Law International: 577-591.

Hussain, Ijaz 1984. *Dissenting and Separate Opinions at the World Court.* Leiden: Martinus Nijhoff Publishing.

Hyland, Ken 1999. Academic attribution: citation and the construction of disciplinary knowledge. *Applied Linguistics* 20(3): 341-367.

International Centre for the Settlement of Investment Disputes 2006. *ICSID Convention Regulations and Rules.*

Martin, James R. / White, Peter R. R. 2004. *The Language of Evaluation: Appraisal in English*. Basingstoke: Palgrave Macmillan.

Sanders, Pieter 1999. *Quo Vadis Arbitration?: Sixty Years of Arbitration Practice: A Comparative Study.* The Hague: Kluwer Law International.

Scheuer, Christoph 2001. *The ICSID Convention: A Commentary.* Cambridge: Cambridge University Press.

Swales, John M. 1990. *Genre Analysis: English in Academic and Research Settings*. Cambridge: Cambridge University Press.

Wangelin, James D. 2004. Buttressing the pillars of arbitration. *Mealey's International Arbitration Report* 19: 1–12.

Weidemaier, W. Mark C. 2010. Toward a theory of precedent in arbitration. *William and Mary Law Review* 51: 1895-1958.

White, Peter R. R. 2003. Beyond modality and hedging: a dialogic view of the language of intersubjective stance. *Text* 23(2): 259-284.

—. 2012. The Appraisal webpage. Consulted 1 August 2012 on: http://grammatics.com/appraisal/index.html

Cases

1. Asante. Asian Agricultural Products Limited v. Democratic Socialist Republic of Sri Lanka (ICSID Case No. ARB/87/3) Dissenting opinion of Samuel K. B. Asante.
2. Berman. Industria Nacional de Alimentos, S.A. and Indalsa Perú, S.A. (formerly Empresas Lucchetti, S.A. and Lucchetti Peru, S.A.) v. Republic of Peru (ICSID Case No. ARB/03/4) Dissenting opinion of Franklin Berman.
3. Born. Biwater Gauff v. United Republic of Tanzania (ICSID Case No. ARB/05/22) Concurring and dissenting opinion of Gary Born.

4. Covarrubias. Marvin Roy Feldman Karpa v. United Mexican States (ICSID Case No. ARB(AF)/99/1) Dissenting opinion of Jorge Covarrubias Bravo.
5. Czar. Sociedad Anónima Eduardo Vieira v. Republic of Chile (ICSID Case No. ARB/04/7) Dissenting opinion of Susana B. Czar de Zalduendo.
6. Highet. Waste Management, Inc. v. United Mexican States (ICSID Case No. ARB(AF)/98/2) Dissenting opinion of Keith Highet.
7. Lalonde. Sempra Energy International v. Argentine Republic (ICSID Case No. ARB/02/16) Partial dissenting opinion of Marc Lalonde.
8. Lowenfeld. Corn Products International, Inc. v. United Mexican States (ICSID Case No. ARB/AF/04/1). Dissenting opinion of Andreas Lowenfeld.
9. Nabulsi. Hussein Nuaman Soufraki v. United Arab Emirates (ICSID Case No. ARB/02/7). Dissenting opinion of Omar Nabulsi.
10. Price. Tokios Tokeles v. Ukraine (ICSID Case No. ARB/02/18) Dissenting opinion of Daniel Price.
11. Rovine. Archer Daniels Midland Company and Tate & Lyle Ingredients Americas, Inc. v. United Mexican States (ICSID Case No. ARB(AF)/04/5) Concurring opinion of Arthur W. Rovine.
12. Suratgar. Mihaly International Corporation v. Democratic Socialist Republic of Sri Lanka (ICSID Case No. ARB/00/2) Concurring opinion of David Suratgar.
13. Weil. Tokios Tokeles v. Ukraine (ICSID Case No. ARB/02/18) Dissenting opinion of Prosper Weil on Decision of Jurisdiction.
14. de Witt. African Holding Company of America, Inc. and Société Africaine de Construction au Congo S.A.R.L. v. Democratic Republic of the Congo (ICSID Case No. ARB/05/21) Dissenting opinion of Otto L.O. de Witt Wijnen.

CHAPTER SEVEN

A QUESTION OF TRAINING: ISSUES OF LANGUAGE AND POWER IN FORMAL POLICE INVESTIGATIVE INTERVIEWS[1]

BRONWEN HUGHES
AND ANTONELLA NAPOLITANO

> "The activity of questioning must stand as one of the most basic and ubiquitous activities engaged in by our social species."
> —Raymond 2003: 961

Introduction

Up to the late 18th century, the Justices of Peace in England and Wales carried out both inquisitorial and magisterial duties. When they later lost their inquisitorial responsibilities, the police force, by default, took over responsibility for this task. It was not, however, until the mid-1980s that any form of guidance for police officers on how to conduct interviews was provided. Such guidance was largely a consequence of the numerous high-profile miscarriages of justice which occurred throughout the 1970s. In the early eighties, a Royal Commission on Criminal Procedure was set up and in 1984 the Police and Criminal Evidence Act, known as PACE was passed. Although the PACE act did in fact delineate the legal boundaries within which police interviewing could be conducted, it did not provide a clear interviewing model which could serve to train investigative officers and guarantee 'best practice'. It was only in 1991 that the Home Office drew up such a model which became known by its mnemonic PEACE,

[1] Although both authors Antonella Napolitano and Bronwen Hughes worked on the entire paper, the part from the beginning of the paper to section II (excluded) is to be attributed to Antonella Napolitano. Section II (included) to the end of the paper is to be attributed to Bronwen Hughes.

each letter of the acronym standing for a separate stage in the five-step interviewing procedure. Post-PEACE interviews were, however, still considered by many to be too coercive and suspects' rights were still not felt to be safeguarded. In the nineties, the Enhanced Cognitive interviewing model was devised, and though it is widely felt that there is still room for improvement, it is the current investigative interviewing model in England and Wales.

This chapter focuses on a number of interviews conducted within the Enhanced Cognitive interview framework. Analysis is carried out upon a number of police training interviews conducted by the Metropolitan Police at the Hendon Police Academy in the United Kingdom. Formal police interviews, together with other types of institutional interviews, are characterised by a dyadic, asymmetrical turn-taking system whose main feature is that of pre-allocation: questions are put forward by the investigating officer(s), answers are provided by the layperson. An investigative interview can be classified as an "elicitation interview" or "information interview" (Shuy 1997: 178), and the questions asked can be placed in two broad categories: information-seeking and confirmation-seeking. As for the answers provided by the layperson in the course of the interview, they can deploy a number of characteristic features: an answer may qualify as a response rather than an answer proper; overt and covert evasion strategies may be adopted in order not to provide the required information; "non type-conforming answers" (Raymond 2003: 947) and "stepwise transition" (Sacks in Jefferson 1984: 196) may be employed in order to furnish extraneous information, and the speaker's epistemic stance may be purposefully called into play to rival that of the investigating officer. Drawing upon the corpus of written transcripts of formal police training interviews and exploiting the methodological framework offered by Conversation Analysis, the key features of these prototypical investigative interviews are identified and analysed.

Corpus

The corpus is made up of 15 advanced suspect interviews for Tier 3 (Specialist Suspect Interviewers) carried out at the Metropolitan Police Crime Academy. The interviews take place on the last day of a three-week training period. The trainee police officers are all detectives whose role "involves serious or complex areas of crime or other critical incidents" (*National Investigative Interviewing Strategy* 2009). The detectives have previously been through Tier 1 (Foundation) and Tier 2 (Dedicated investigator) training. The two interviewing officers present in the interview room (interviewer and transcriber) are provided with what is known as a "Scenario Pack" which contains statements from victims and eyewitnesses. The actors who impersonate the suspect in each interview also only have access to the "Scenario Pack". The interview is entirely improvised, no scripts are provided. The suspects present in the corpus interviews have been arrested for alleged arson, sexual assault, grievous bodily harm, drug handling and both first and second degree murder. During the course of the interview, the Tier 3 trainees are being monitored in "real time" by a group of Tier 5 National Interview Advisors present on the premises. To all intents and purposes this is a pass/fail exam situation. Should the trainees fail, they maintain their Tier 2 status and can therefore continue interviewing suspects for what is known as "volume crime" or "non-strategic crime", but they will not at this stage become specialist suspect interviewers.

Methodology

The audio-visual interviews provided by the Metropolitan Police Crime Academy have been transcribed using Jefferson's (2004) transcription model. They have then been investigated by means of a conversation analytical framework applied to "institutional talk" (Heritage 2005). Particular attention has been given to the structure of the asymmetrical formal interview, the pre-allocation of turns, question typology and third turn receipt markers. A specific aim of the investigation has been to illustrate the manner in which, by means of the "conversationalization" of discourse (Fairclough 1996) and "synthetic personalization" devices (Fairclough 2001), friendship and intimacy, emotions commonly associated with ordinary or mundane conversation, become an integral part of institutional discourse. Indeed, the exploitation of these emotions serves to forward the goals of the police institution. The boundary between "ordinary" and "institutional" talk is thus blurred and one could even claim that in the police interview setting, goal-oriented mundane talk becomes institutional.

Research objectives

The interviews present in our corpus would at first sight appear to be as canonical as Enhanced Cognitive Interviews (ECI) (see the investigative interview: background information below) can possibly be, in that not only have the investigating officers just completed a three-week training course but they are also being actively monitored throughout the interview procedure and, as previously mentioned, are under considerable pressure to succeed in becoming Tier 3 specialist interviewers. We would, however, posit that a number of features (excessive neutrality in the third turn receipt markers denoting a total lack of empathy, fictitious conversationalisation devices, inability to adhere to an open-question TEDS model, see below) illustrate that certain coercive, pre-ECI mechanisms still live on, and one may indeed wonder whether such mechanisms gain ground when the investigative interviews are part of routine police work and not scripted activities.

The investigative interview

Background information

In England, Wales and Northern Ireland, the mid- and late 1970s were characterised by a number of clamorous miscarriages of justice which mainly involved IRA crimes. In widely-publicised judicial cases such as *the Birmingham Six* and *the Guildford Four* the culprits were initially sentenced to life imprisonment only to have the verdict subsequently overturned when excessively coercive interview techniques, the manipulation of evidence, and the often fallacious re-wording of witness/suspect statements came to light.

The search for a fair investigative interviewing procedure led to the Police and Criminal Evidence Act (PACE) (1984 c. 60). Along with other obligatory procedural rulings, *PACE* stipulated that:

- all formal interviews should be tape-recorded;
- all suspects should be cautioned at the time of arrest.

Although the *PACE* act did, at least apparently, define the legislative boundaries within which investigative interviewing should be conducted, it did not in fact delineate an interviewing model which could serve to train police officers and standardise the practice of interviewing. In 1992 the Home Office drew up such a model, which soon became known by its mnemonic *P.E.A.C.E.*:

- **P**: planning and preparation
- **E**: engage and explain
- **A**: account
- **C**: closure
- **E:** evaluation

Despite considerable improvement in interviewing techniques, post-P.E.A.C.E. interviews were still considered to be too coercive (Baldwin 1993, Milne and Bull 1999), a rapport was not established with the suspect, witness or victim, questions were of the proof elicitation type and, in general, investigative interviews were still conducted in an excessively forceful manner. Throughout the eighties and early nineties the *Cognitive Interview* (CI) model was developed (Geiselman et al. 1984), followed shortly afterwards by the *Enhanced Cognitive Interview* (ECI), which included the four original cognitive components proper to the Cognitive Interview but added a number of *Conversation Management* (CM) *skills:*

1) Cognitive Components:
    - mental context reinstatement (encoding specificity: thoughts, emotions, smells etc.)
    - report everything (no editing of details)
    - recall in a variety of temporal orders (gist retrieval, start from end or beginning of event)
    - change perspective (adopt the perspective of another person)

2) Conversational Management/Communication Skills (Dando and Milne 2009).

   Before introducing the four cognitive components (above), the interviewing officers must:
    - establish rapport by asking innocuous and easily answered questions – they must use no jargon – they must underline that the interviewee's efforts dictate the (successful/unsuccessful) outcome of the interview;
    - tailor their questions according to a witness's pattern of recall rather than a rigid sequence of requests for information ("interrogation" style);
    - use open-ended questions with strategic pauses and without interruptions;
    - use guided imagery, ask the interviewee to evoke mental images.

The Enhanced Cognitive Interview, which brings together the four core cognitive components of the Cognitive interview together with the conversation management skills listed above, is, within the P.E.A.C.E framework, the interviewing model presently employed by police forces in England, Wales and Northern Ireland. As regards question typology, both excessively coercive confirmation and information questions of the type illustrated in Figure 7-1 below are discouraged in favour of the so-called "TEDS" model of open, non-threatening questions. The TEDS acronym is a mnemonic which is helpful when formulating open questions. It stands for Tell, Explain, Describe, Show.

The following are examples of open questions which follow the TEDS model:

- ***Tell*** me about what happened next…
- I'd like you to ***explain*** why you did that…
- Can you ***describe*** what you did next …
- *Show* me where you were standing…

In general, interviewing officers are required to adhere to a neutral, non-judgemental frame of questioning. Long, accusatory or disjunctive questions are frowned upon, as is the use of sarcasm or snubbing devices.

Macro-functions	
Confirmation-seeking questions	Information-seeking questions
Micro-functions	
Declarative plus tag as request for agreement	Open information-seeking questions
Tag questions	*Wh-* questions
Bare declaratives	Polar alternatives
	Either/or questions

Figure 7-1 Confirmation/information-seeking questions

Interview structure

The interviews making up the corpus present all the canonical features of institutional interviews. They are dyadic and asymmetrical with pre-allocated turns: the interviewer asks the questions and the interviewee, in this case the suspect, answers. The "dominance" of the professional incumbent is manifested through various aspects: his/her right to first turn position in the question/answer sequence, his/her management of the topical agenda, his/her management of the third turn.

> Anyone in the position of answering is restricted to dealing with just what is asked in the prior question: though the question may be understood in the light of what has come before, and what is anticipated to be in the line of questioning being developed, nevertheless it is the prior question which demands to be answered (Drew and Heritage 1992: 506).

The aim of the *TEDS* model for question typology is to level out the standard asymmetrical structure of the investigative interview, awarding both suspect and interviewing officer equal, or as close to equal as possible, discursive rights.

There are, however, occasions in which the suspect in her/his second turn will put forward a question. As is evident in the following excerpts, s/he will only "be allowed" to do so when there is a genuine breakdown in communication. Should s/he initiate questioning in order to seek out common ground with the investigating officer or to express a polemic or belligerent attitude, the officer will avoid any form of accommodation. In the case where common ground is sought, the investigating officer will call upon "generalized" cases (Extreme Case Formulations) (Pomerantz 1986) which do not imply personal involvement, and when the suspect asks polemical or belligerent questions "out of turn", the officer will merely postpone his/her answering turn until s/he has reached the appropriate point in a pre-established agenda.

The research[2]

I. Suspect-initiated questions

a) Requests for clarification

1)	I.O:	((open-handed gesture, palms upturned)) Ok↓ °thank you for that° (.) Sam↑ (0.2) tell me what you know- tell me what you di- what happened yesterday↑ (.) last night↓
	→S:	We::ll (.) wh-what d'you mean (.) which bit↑
2)	I.O:	Ok↓ (.) so tell me about the route you took↑ >what route did you take↑<
	→S:	I wen- I don't- (.) what d'you mean↑
3)	I.O:	Ok↓ so tell me about what happened- (.) tell me what happened- when did you- when you met her at the bar↑
	→S:	Now I've (.) we:ll what- what d'you want to know↑ (0.5) I-I don't understand↓
4)	I.O:	Tell me about- (0.5) >what- when you were at the station↓<
	→S:	((agitated, lifting hands up and down)) Well I- (.) I don't understand (.) I mean we're here (.) what difference does that

[2] In all the quoted excerpts the initials "I.O" stand for Investigating Officer and "S" stands for Suspect. In all excerpts italics have been used by authors to draw attention to specific parts of the text.

		make↑ I mean (.) YOU'RE at the station↓ so we know what the station's about↑
5)	I.O:	((open handed, palms up, conciliating gesture)) Ok↓ I'm just trying to clarify (.) to give you a new opportunity to tell your version of events=
	→S:	=Well wha::t↑ what is it you're asking about↓ I don't understand=
6)	I.O:	Ok↓ and (0.5) so y've- (.) y've arrived home uhh (0.2) tell me what time you got home↑ >when did you get home↑<
	→S:	Mate↓ what do↑- (.) what can↑ (0.2) I don't remember what time it was (.) I mean this is all like (.) between one o'clock 'nd maybe two-two thirty (.) I don't know↑
7)	I.O:	So↓ ((back of left hand hits palm of right)) it's about six-thirty (.) you said it's about (.) four policemen in your room↓ they got you out of bed↓ ((still 'beating' back of left hand on palm of right)) you didn't- you were pretty unsure what's going on↓ (0.5) tell me about the arrest itself↓ what did the police say to you↑
	→S:	Ah (.) what did-↑ (0.5) when↑(.) (I) can't remember mate (.) it was like (0.5) it was just all- all- (.) well my head was spinning >I don't know what was going on< so I can't remember what they said↓

Certain conversational utterances are strictly interrelated and interdependent. The term "adjacency pairs" is used to refer to these paired actions which constitute the primary resource for organising courses of action in spoken discourse. Adjacency pairs in their most basic, unexpanded form are made up of two turns each produced by a different speaker. These turns are usually produced adjacently and can be differentiated into first pair parts and second pair parts. The two parts are type-related: question/answer, offer/acceptance or refusal, greeting/return greeting and so on.

In a conversation analytical framework, the organisation of preference "refers to the institutionalized methods speakers use for managing and producing affiliative and disaffiliative actions and their aggregate consequences" (Raymond 2003: 942). When acting in an affiliative manner, the speaker will provide the expected preferred response in his/her second turn (an answer to a question, a counter-greeting upon being greeted), whereas when acting in a disaffiliative manner, s/he will put forward a dispreferred second pair part.

In all seven of the above excerpts, the suspect is visibly aware of the fact that he is producing a dispreferred response: in excerpts 1, 4 and 5 he fronts his answer with “well”, as a hedging or mitigating device to postpone confrontation. In extracts 2 and 3 he initially attempts to provide a preferred response and answer the question, only to then break down and ask for clarification, clearly a dispreferred option. In examples 6 and 7, he again asks for clarification but softens his dispreferred response by using the term “mate” as an ingratiatory device.

This first set of examples illustrates that the suspect is well aware of his role as “respondent” within the institutional question/answer chain characterised by turn pre-allocation. Not wishing to provide dispreferred second pair parts, he attempts to adopt a number of ingratiatory tactics.

We will now pursue our investigation by observing the manner in which the investigative officer reacts when the suspect deliberately chooses to behave in a disaffiliative way and provide a dispreferred question in his allocated turn.

b) polemic enquiries

8)	I.O:	=Ok↓ Well now you’ve told me that you smoke↓ well now you (.) drink lager or drink beer and you like a=
	→S:	=WHAT’S WRONG WITH THAT↑
	I.O:	There’s nothing wrong with that Sam↓ it’s just (that) I’m trying to get=
	→S:	=what’s that got to do with anything↓ do <u>you</u> drink and smoke↑
	I.O:	U::h (0.2) I- I don’t drink↓ however (.) *people dri::nk* ((hands reach out from chest with palms upturned)) I’m just trying to get a picture of you so (0.5) uhh (.) it’s not a trick (0.2) so↓ let’s go back to you (.)
9)	I.O:	((hands open resting on knees, palms upwards)) Ok↓ (.) >‘nd you said (that)< you went to sleep when you eventually could (.) ‘nd you woke up in the [night-]
	→S:	[No] (.) isn’t that what you do↑
	I.O:	((hands open, palms upwards)) we *all-* (0.2)that’s *what everybody does*↓ (.) ‘nd you wake up in the night (.) tell me about that (.) when-

In the two extracts above, the suspect reacts to the investigative officer's questions in a particularly belligerent manner, he attempts to step out of his pre-allocated respondent role and take over the first pair part questioner's role, thus calling into play the investigating officer on a personal level.

Besides the pre-allocated turn-taking framework and the consequent preference organisation, a further basic tenet of interview discourse is that of the institutional representative's neutral stance. The interviewer, particularly in the case of police interviews does not act or speak on his/her own behalf; s/he represents and forwards the aims and opinions of an institution. Thus, s/he does not take up an individual role but an institutional one. The interviewer's neutral stance is determined by the fact that as the representative of an institution, s/he does not stand as the primary recipient of the interview proceedings. Such a role is embodied by an "overhearing audience". In the case of formal police interviews, the terms "overhearing audience" are employed to define the entire judicial apparatus of which the investigative interview is an initial though integral part and for which the audio tapes used throughout the interview stand as a proxy. Should the tapes testify to the fact that the investigative interview was not carried out in a neutral, non-coercive manner, the subsequent steps along the judicial ladder (the court hearing, the sentencing and possible imprisonment) would be severely jeopardised. Thus the role of the judicial apparatus as an "overhearing audience" serves to ensure that the interviewer maintains his/her formal, institutional stance and refrains from expressing personal views or opinions.

In the scripted training interviews which make up our corpus the investigating officer needs to maintain his/her neutral stance, not only because of the overriding institutional framework, but also because s/he is being closely monitored by the Tier 5 Interview Advisors.

In the excerpts above, the investigating officer uses extreme case formulations (ECF) to avoid personal accountability and maintain his/her neutral stance when answering the suspect's polemic questions.

> Interactants use extreme-case formulations when they anticipate or expect their co-interactants to undermine their claims and when they are in adversarial situations (Pomerantz 1986: 222).

By calling into play a general or objective situation, the detective manages to avoid involvement on a personal level. When asked whether he drinks (example 8 above), he initially provides a hesitant personal response: "I-I don't drink" only to then turn to the more general ECF "people drink". In example 9 above, he again avoids personal involvement by stating "we all- that's what everybody does".

In the next part of our investigation, we will look at a third type of suspect-initiated questions: after genuine incomprehension and polemic intent, we are now dealing with examples of information-seeking questions. Again we are faced with instances in which the suspect steps out of his pre-allocated second turn respondent role and interferes with the investigative officer's pre-established agenda. Due to the considerable length of these excerpts and space restrictions we will merely indicate the missing turns.

c) Information-seeking questions

10)	→S:	((belligerent tone)) =*why am I here*↑
	I.O:	Ok↓(.) well↓ I'll explain everything to you Clive (.) my name's Glen Be[rry]
	→S:	((very belligerent))[*nobo*]*dy's told me why I'm here*↑
	I.O:	Ok Clive↓ (.) *I'm going to explain to you why you're here* (0.5) my name's Glen Berry (.) I'm a detective and I'm based here at this police station >which is Hendon< ((points to floor, left hand, with tapping gesture when he says Hendon)) (0.5) this chap sat behind you is Tom ((stretches out left arm in sweeping gesture towards the transcribing officer, to his left))
		[28 turns elapse]
	→S:	*[well I wonder] why you've got me here (.) you've not been telling me why I'm here*↑
		[5 turns elapse]
11)	→I.O:	=and the last part of the caution is that anything you do say can be given in evidence >that means< ((gestures with left arm outstretched towards tape recorder)) that the tapes from this interview can be played at court↓ (0.5) now (.) *you're here* because you've been arrested on suspicion of murder↑ (.) ok↑ (.) murder is when one person intends to hurt another person and kills him↓
		[33 turns elapse before interviewing officer answers suspect's original question]

	→S:	*WHO SAID IT WAS ME ANYway* (.) who thought it was me↑
	I.O:	=ok↓ ((hands stretched out, palms upwards)) <we're going to talk about everything in a second Clive > ok↓ erhm we're going to talk about <u>you</u> ((sticks out thumb of left hand and "counts 1" with it by clutching it with right hand)) (.) we're going to talk about where you were (.) erhm
	→S:	=*was it a policeman*↑
	I.O:	=we're going to talk about- ((hesitates, looks around blankly, seems confused))
	→S:	=*WAS IT a policeman*↑
	I.O:	=I'm going to explain to you- (('counts 2' on index finger of left hand by clutching it with right hand))
	→S:	=*it was*↓ *wasn't it*↑
	I.O:	I- I (.) >I'm sorry Clive< (0.5) what was a police officer↑
	→S:	=*who's making out they saw me*↑
	I.O:	A po::lice officer who saw you leaving the address↑
	→S:	=what you just said (.) yeah↓
	I.O:	No:: (.) I-I (.)***I****'ll-* ***we****'ll get into that in a second* Clive (0.5) ok↓ ((counts 1 on left hand again)) so I'd like to talk about <u>you</u> (.) ((counts 2 by clutching index of left hand with fingers of right)) where you were on Saturday the 18th from 7pm until- a(t)- you were arrested on Sunday morning [of the 19th of March]

In excerpt 11 above, the suspect never obtains an answer to his question as it evidently contravenes the investigating officer's pre-established agenda and would probably lead the detective to disclose evidence to which the suspect is not entitled.

In the same example, it is interesting to note the investigating officer's evident discomfort and his switch, in the final turn of excerpt 11 above, from the 1st person singular "I" pronoun to the 1st person plural "we". The use of *we* in this case could have either an inclusive function (to mean the investigating officer + the suspect) or, possibly, a more exclusive, institutional function, to denote the officers present in the room: investigating officer and transcribing officer, and therefore the police institution itself.

Despite the democratisation of interview procedure and the Conversation Management skills now included in the Enhanced Cognitive Interview, it must be remembered that the *when*, *where* and *how* of the interview are established by the police institution, as is the agenda to be followed throughout. The investigating officer also finds himself in an "accrued knowledge state" (Heydon 2005: 83) as he has access to the transcripts of victim and witness testimony. Thus, when the suspect asks a (usually polemical) question which interferes with the investigating officer's established agenda, such questions are usually ignored or, at best, considerably postponed.

In the context of taped and/or audio recorded investigative interviews, where the tape or audio recording serves as an "overhearing audience", and can later be used in court to prove veracity, the interviewer avoids the role of news-recipient and primary addressee by abstaining from producing "acknowledgment tokens" such as "good" (Jefferson 1984: 198), news-marks such as "oh really?" or "did you?" (Jefferson 1981: 15). Within the enhanced cognitive interview framework, however, interviewing officers are encouraged to create rapport, to personalise the suspect/police officer relationship and to empathise with the suspect.

In the second part of our investigation we will attempt to illustrate that, despite the relatively new guidelines born out of the merging of the cognitive interview model and a number of conversation management strategies which strongly encourage rapport-building and empathy, the traditional institutional neutral stance is so ingrained that even at times in which the suspect is extremely agitated or upset, the interviewing officer will systematically employ the neutral un-empathetic third turn receipt marker "ok" with descending intonation.

II. Third turn receipt markers

a) Neutral "ok" as a receipt marker

12)	S:	=I wasn't ready you know↓ and it was all a bit too much for me (.) and she was more pissed than I thought- she was↓- >so it was like↓< ((left hand up in front, shoulder height in "keep away" gesture)) pffffff:: she was on her feet when I sa- >I got up↓ she got up↓< (.) and I just said pfff::: ((hands up in front, shoulder height, in "keep away" gesture)) I'm not into that (.) can't remember what I said (0.5) (I) just got off 'nd left her there↓ (I) didn't=
	→I.O:	=Ok↓
13)	S:	((stretches out both hands to left in "pulling up" gesture)) I go to get her hands↓ to get- ((quoting voice, girly and high-pitched)) "come on- come on" to help her up (.) she's giggling↓ I put my hands out↓ she grabs my right hand↓ and puts it straight on her tit ((puts right hand on left breast area)) I didn't- (.) I wasn't=
	→I.O:	=Ok↓

14)	S:	No↓ (.) no::↑ fucking hell I wasn't thinking about anything else↑ I was thinking about what the fucking hell I was going to do↑ >one minute I was- I'm having a kiss 'nd cuddle with the girl< thinking she's playing hide 'nd seek from her mate↓ next minute she's sticking me ha::nd down her knickers↑
	→I.O:	Ok↓
15)	S:	Erhm (.) well I stayed in the room (.) erhm (I) had a few drinks (.) I was watching telly erhm (.) 'nd that was about it↓ (0.5) and then Michelle called (0.2) so she said she wanted to come over (.) and- 'nd I said yeah all right 'nd then we had like a few drinks in the bar (.) >down at the bottom of the hotel< (.) 'nd then we went back up to the room and >that's when< she went crazy- (.) she started going nuts- I didn't- I wasn't=
	→I.O:	=Ok↓

b) Formulations with lexical variation

A further discursive strategy commonly employed in institutional interviews and present in the excerpts from our corpus consists in the use of formulations. The term "formulation" was coined by Conversation Analysis researchers to describe utterances that "[s]ummarise, gloss, or develop the gist of the recipient's earlier contributions" (Heritage 1985: 103).

Whereas in mundane conversation formulations are commonly used to provide a "summary" of prior talk for the purposes of clarification, and necessarily contain different words and phrases from the original, as a demonstration of comprehension by the producer of the formulation, in investigative interviews "[f]ormulations are used to create the illusion that the police version is really only a summary of the suspect's version with some changes that may be required for clarification by the police interviewer" (Heydon 2005: 140).

Fairclough notes that formulations "have a controlling function and provide a way of leading participants into accepting one's own version of what has transpired, and so limiting their options for future contributions" (Fairclough 2001: 136). Thus, formulations serve to forward an adversarial response in the third turn position of the turn–taking sequence while at the same time maintaining the professional incumbent's neutral stance and the overhearing audience's status as primary recipient: "[…] a formulation can be used to resist or challenge what an interviewee has to say while maintaining the stance of formal neutrality" (Heritage 1985: 114).

In excerpts 16 and 17 quoted below, taken from our corpus of Metropolitan Police training interviews, formulations with lexical variation are employed when the actions taken by police officers are mentioned. When summing up the information provided by the suspect, the investigating officer converts the strong terms employed (*dragged, shoved, grabbed, shocked*) into far weaker terms (*put, got, pretty unsure*), and, in excerpt 16, he employs the passive voice to mitigate accountability and make the police officers less answerable for their actions. By lexically minimising the suspect's account of events, the interviewing officer effectively removes the notion of excessive police force and by doing so considerably modifies the suspect's version of events.

16)	I.O:	Ok↓ (0.5) so (.) ((“counts” by putting back of left hand into right palm)) the police who arrested you (0.2) >tell me about what actually happened< after they actually arrested you↓
	S:	We::ll (.) they dragged me down (.) they shoved me in the van (.) ‘nd then brought me here
	3rd turn→I.O:	So↓ ((back of left hand against right palm)) the police arrested you↓ you were put in a van↓ ‘nd brought to the station↓
17)	I.O:	Ok↓ obviously (the) police were arresting you↓ what happened↑ (0.5) at that poin- when you were arrested↑
	S:	(I) don't know >it's just like< they just *grabbed* me↓ I didn't know what it was about↓ I had no idea what was going on↓ (I'd) I was fast asleep (.) >you know< (.) (I'd) hhhh. It was like↓ I kinda struggled a bit ‘cos >it's like what's going on↑< *it was quite a shock*↑ I-I was *shocked* you know >I didn't mean to cause any trouble< but it's like (.) >you know< (0.5) I was fast asleep > ‘nd suddenly I'm *being dragged* out of bed by (the) police so- < (.) so (.) yeah↓
	3rd turn→I.O:	So↓ ((back of left hand on palm of right)) it's about six-thirty (.) it's about- (.) > policemen in your room↓< they *got* you out of bed↓ ((still “counting” back of left hand on palm of right)) you didn't- you were *pretty unsure* ‘bout what's going on↓

III. Lack of open-question TEDS model

Within the Enhanced Cognitive Interview, the elicitation of information from the suspect should be obtained by means of wide-reaching open-ended questions which follow the witness's or suspect's pattern of recall. Rigid "interrogation style" sequences of *wh*- information-seeking questions are actively discouraged as they interrupt the witness/victim/suspect's memory recall flow and constrain her/him to fit into a pre-established framework set by the investigating officer.

> For example, the interviewer should both allow and encourage the interviewee to do the majority of the talking by the use of open ended questions wherever possible and the strategic use of pauses. [...] Indeed, open-ended questions (e.g. tell me everything about the robbery) are associated with longer response latencies (longer time spent thinking before answering) compared to specific closed questions (e.g. those that tend to start with what, where, when etc.). This suggests that, when asked an open question, interviewees may well be conducting a more detailed and thorough memory search. (Dando / Milne 2009: 157)

Despite the fact that they have just attended an intensive three week training course and are actively undergoing observed interview training, in the investigative interviews which make up our corpus, the interviewing officers systematically appear unable to remain within the *TEDS* framework and regularly revert to asking *wh*- questions. Although *wh*-questions, as opposed to polar interrogatives, allow the suspect greater freedom to produce more than a yes/no answer, the amount of information the respondent can produce in a reply to these types of question in an investigative interview is still constrained by the questioner and by the question he has formulated. As Gibbons (2003: 101) remarks: "The more information included in the question, the greater the questioner's control of the information, so the answerer can contribute less new information".

Wh- questions restrict the respondent's answer to the specific aspect (and exclusively that aspect) specified by the interrogative pronoun: "Where did you first meet the victim?" Here the questioner is not interested in the "when", "how" or "who" of the situation, but merely on the "where": thus the constraint put upon the respondent not to discursively organise and narrate his own "free" version of events is considerable.

In the following excerpts taken from a variety of interviews which make up our corpus, the interviewing officers manifest great difficulty in remaining within the "tell me" framework and automatically revert to *wh*-questions, which belong to a more "interrogation" style of interviewing:

18)	→I.O:	Ok↓ Let's (.) take it back a little (.) a stage further (0.5) *tell me*- (.) let's start from (.) coming back to what happened yesterday afternoon leading up to what you did yesterday afternoon (.) say from 6 pm yesterday↓ (.) so:: (0.2) *what did*- (.)*where we::r*- *what were you doing* at 6 pm yesterday↑
19)	→I.O:	Ok↓ (0.5) well tell me- (0.5) *tell me* where you- *where* were- *where were you* on Saturday↑
20)	→I.O:	Ok↓ (1.5) so I want to fo::cus on the evening part of Saturday now (.) ok (.) ('nd) you told me that you were wandering around into the evening (.) *tell me* more about the evening of (your) day (0.2) where did- (.) *tell me*- (.) *what did you do on Saturday evening*↑
21)	→I.O:	*Tell me* where- (.) where you were going to go in the taxi erhm- *tell me* about that conversation↑ did you- *what was* the result of it↑ *what did you say*↑ In the above excerpt, notice the increasingly specific question content
22)	→I.O:	*Tell me* about (.) why you think your hand °may have gone° inside- *why did* you thi::- *why did* your hand- (0.5) °go inside her knickers° In moving from the "tell me" framework, and trying to find a suitable question structure, the interviewing officer ends up asking a completely different question and moves from an information-seeking frame to an accusatory frame with pre-supposition in the question content.

IV. When conversationalisation becomes institutional

When marking the difference between "institutional talk" and "mundane" or ordinary conversation, Drew / Heritage (1992: 22) laid down two foundational tenets:

> Institutional interaction may often involve special and particular constraints on what one or both of the participants will treat as allowable contributions to the business at hand […] institutional interaction involves an orientation by at least one of the participants to some core goal, task or identity […] conventionally associated with the institution in question.

As regards the "particular constraints" which participants adhere to, our investigation of suspect-initiated questions, and the repeated use of neutral third turn receipt markers, illustrates that both the interviewing officer and the suspect are fully aware of their discourse roles in the asymmetrical, dyadic, pre-allocated turn-taking system of the investigative interview.

As for the "task", or "goal-orientation" of institutional discourse, we wish to posit that due to the "democratization" of discourse imposed by the enhanced cognitive interview framework, in which "rapport building" is one of the dominant features, mundane conversation becomes an integral part of institutional discourse as it is:

- present exclusively within the investigative interviewer initiated turns (1st and 3rd).
- strongly goal-oriented and forwards the aims of the interviewer.

Though referring to company-initiated telephone sales, we cannot but agree with Alice Freed when she states: "Changes that are occurring in many customer-service institutions, accompanied as they are by modifications in the type of talk that takes place within them, provide us with grounds for broadening our view of institutional talk" (Freed 2010: 318).

In the following excerpts, mundane "friendly" talk is an integral part of the interview framework:

23)	→I.O:	As I said I'm a detective↓ and erhm (.) *my job here* in this interview is *to do everything I can (.) t- to try and he- help* <u>*you*</u> to tell me what's happened↓
24)	→I.O:	*=is it ok if we call you Tony↑ (.) ok↓ thank you Tony↓* (.) erhm (0.2) now when you were brought into the police station↓ (.) (I) think it was late last night↓ [missing text due to space constraints] that is something you can do throughout *your stay* with us and throughout this interview↓ (do) you understand that↑

		In the above excerpt notice the lack of reciprocity in the use of Christian names and the euphemistic use of the term “stay”.
25)	→I.O:	E:rhm (0.2) as I said it (0.5) this *is your time* (.) it’s *your opportunity*↓ it’s *your interview* today erhm (.) ‘nd *I hope- I do hope that we’ll be able to do erhm (.) everything we can to get you to tell us* what happened last night↓ erhm (.)
		Here, notice the contradiction between the friendly, empathetic “hope we’ll be able to do” and the coercive “get you to”.
26)	→I.O:	(And) as I said *this is your interview*↓ (.) [missing text due to time constraints] now there are a number of things I want to talk to you about this- the why you’ve been brought here er- *I want to talk to you today*↓ *(.) I’d like to talk to you today (.) I’d like you to talk to me a little bit about yourself*↓ *(.) I would like you to talk to me* about the time yesterday evening at the Farmer’s Arms Pub↓
		In the above excerpt notice the repair from “me to you” to “you to me”.
27)	→I.O:	There you go Sam (.) take a seat there please↓ ((stretches arm out laterally towards chair positioned opposite I.O’s chair – Loud buzzing of tape as recorder is switched on)) Sam (.) that buzzing noise you can hear shows the tapes are working (0.2) everything in this room is now being recorded (.) ok↑ (0.5) >we’re now going to explain a few things to you< (.) we’re now going to explain to you what will happen to the tapes (0.5) *so you’ve been calling me Andy* (.) you *have to* continue with that (.) *we have to* continue being called first names ((hand gesture from I.O’s chest out and back)) (.) Andy and Sam↓
		Here the use of deontic “have to” points to an external institutional obligation

Conclusion

On the basis of the results of our investigation which, it must be remembered, takes into account a corpus of 15 Metropolitan Police training interviews, we would posit that a number of features – the excessively strict adherence to a pre-established agenda, marked neutrality in the third turn receipt markers denoting a lack of empathy, fictitious conversationalisation devices employed for institutional aims, and the apparent inability to adhere to an open-question *TEDS* framework – illustrate that certain coercive, pre-enhanced cognitive interview mechanisms still live on. One may indeed wonder whether such mechanisms gain ground when the investigative interviews are no longer mere training sessions.

Recent research in the field of forensic psychology (Dando / Milne 2009, Dando et al. 2011) points to the fact that the enhanced cognitive interview is not well-received by investigative interviewers (especially at Tier 3 level), due to the considerable length of time required for its integral application, which does not tally with institutional time constraints. Research is being carried out to produce a modified, more "user friendly" version of the enhanced cognitive interview.

Basing our judgement on the numerous linguistic features we have observed while carrying out our research, it would seem that a true "democratization" of the investigative interview procedure is and will remain extremely hard to achieve. The intrinsic nature of the suspect/investigating officer interview is necessarily asymmetrical and adversarial as it places the institutional representative and the lay person on opposite sides of the fence, with contrasting goal-orientations: the suspect wishes to evade accountability, the officer needs to collect proof.

It can be said that the Metropolitan Police training interviews do to all effects belong to the realm of fictitious discourse in that the spoken activity which takes place therein is based on invented "scenarios" and therefore stands as a "representation" of the genuine evidentiary police interview, in which discourse is a consolidated form of social practice. As training interviews, however, these scenarios also constitute both a model and a framework for the "genuine" interviews which the Tier 3 detectives will later carry out in the course of their professional duties.

The police interview, whether as a training model or as a consolidated institutional practice, is clearly both intertextual and interdiscursive. Intertextual in that it manifests a plurality of text sources connected to specific bodies of knowledge (the numerous formulaic utterances, the training manuals), and interdiscursive in so far as any characteristic text evokes a particular dominant discoursal value, associated as it is with some institutional and social meaning.

Although the conversational management elements now present in the Enhanced Cognitive Interview would appear to render police evidentiary interviews more "democratic" and less asymmetrical, it must be remembered that they are the end result of a lengthy, in-depth study carried out by the Police institution and other designated research bodies. The ECI therefore stands as a constructed form of practice characterised by enhanced reflexivity (Giddens: 1991) where the construction of the police interview as a practice is in fact produced by its practitioners as part of the practice itself. As Fairclough (1999: 81) states: " […] any reduction of discourse to skills is complicit with efforts on the part of those who have power to impose social practices they favour by getting people to see them as mere techniques."

It must also be said that, besides the verbal resource, the focus of our present investigation, the affordances and constraints of other semiotic modes of communication (space, gaze, gesture, proxemics) must also be taken into consideration and are at present being researched by the authors (results forthcoming). Suffice it to say that in terms of space, the interview room with its structured, pre-established layout is in fact the semiotic embodiment of the activity which takes place therein and "[t]he interpersonal meaning of many types of building is carried by the placing and styling of 'sites of power', that is, a building expresses the political relations between its various users" (O'Toole 2004: 19). Thus, we wish to posit that, despite recent attempts at "democratization", the police interview is and remains a form of dominant discourse which forwards the aims and objectives of a specific institution.

References

ACPO 2009. National Investigative Interviewing Strategy (NIIS), London: ACPO. Available at http://www.npia.police.uk/en/docs/National_Investigative_Interviewing_Strategy_09.pdf.

Baldwin, John 1993. Police interview techniques: establishing truth or proof?. *The British Journal of Criminology* 33(3): 325-352.

Cotterill, Janet (ed.) 2004. *Language in the Legal Process.* Hampshire: Palgrave Macmillan.

Dando, Coral / Milne, Rebecca 2009. Cognitive interviewing. In R. Kocsis (ed.) *AppliedCriminal Psychology: A Guide to Forensic Behavioural Sciences*. Springfield: Charles C. Thomas: 147-168.

Dando, Coral / Wilcock, Rachel / Behnkle, C. / Milne, Rebecca 2011. Modifying the cognitive interview: countenancing forensic application by enhancing practicability. *Psychology Crime and Law* 17(6): 491-511.

Drew, Paul / Heritage, John (eds.) 1992. *Talk at Work: Interaction in Institutional Settings.* Cambridge: Cambridge University Press.

Fairclough, Norman 1996. Technologisation of discourse'. In Caldas-Coulthard, C. / Coulthard, M. (eds.) *Texts and Practices: Readings in Critical Discourse Analysis*. London: Routledge: 71-83.

—. 1999. Global capitalism and critical awareness of language. Available at http://www.cddc.vt.edu/digitalfordism/fordism_materials/fairclough.htm

—. 2001. 2nd edition. *Language and Power.* Essex: Pearson Education Limited.

Freed, Alice 2010. I'm calling to let you know. In *Why Do You Ask? : The Function of Questions in Institutional Discourse*. Oxford: Oxford University Press: 297-321.

Geiselman, R.Edward / Fisher, Ronald P. / Firstenberg, Iris / Hutton, L. A. / Sullivan, S. J. / Avetissian, I. V. / and Prosk, A. L. 1984. Enhancement of eyewitness memory: an empirical evaluation of the cognitive interview. *Journal of Police Science and Administration* 12(1): 74-80.

Gibbons, John 2003. *Forensic Linguistics: an Introduction to Language in the Justice System.* Oxford: Blackwell Publishing Ltd.

Giddens, Anthony 1991. *Modernity and Self-Identity: Self and Society in the Late Modern Age.* Stanford: Stanford University Press.

Heritage, John 1985. Analyzing news interviews: aspects of the production of talk for an overhearing audience. In van Dijk, T. (ed.), *Handbook of Discourse Analysis, vol. 3: Discourse and Dialogue*. London: Academic Press: 95-117.

—. 2005. Conversation analysis and institutional talk. In Fitch, K.L. / Sanders, R.E. (eds.), *Handbook of Language and Social Interaction.* Mahwah, NJ: Lawrence Erlbaum: 103-147.

Heydon, Georgina 2005. *The Language of Police Interviewing: A Critical Analysis.* Hampshire: Palgrave Macmillan.

Jefferson, Gail 1981. The abominable "ne"?: A working paper exploring the phenomenon of post response pursuit of response" (Occasional Paper No.6). Manchester: University of Manchester, Department of Sociology: 1-82.

—. 1984. Notes on a systematic deployment of the acknowledgement tokens "yeah" and "mm hm". *Papers in Linguistics* 17: 197-206.

—. 2004. Glossary of transcript symbols with an introduction. In Lerner, G.H. (ed.) *Conversation Analysis: Studies from the First Generation.* Amsterdam/Philadelphia: John Benjamins: 13-31.

Milne, Rebecca / Bull, Ray 1999. *Investigative Interviewing: Psychology and Practice*. Chichester, England: John Wiley and Sons Ltd.

O'Toole, Michael 2004. Opera Ludentes: the Sydney Opera House at work and play. In O'Halloran, K. L. (ed.), *Multimodal Discourse Analysis*. London/New York: Continuum: 11-54.

Police and Criminal Evidence Act (PACE) and Codes of Practice, document published by the Health and Safety Commission. Available at http://www.hse.gov.uk.

Pomerantz, Anita 1986. Extreme case formulations: a way of legitimizing claims. *Human Studies* 9: 219-229.

Raymond, Geoffrey 2003. Grammar and social organization: yes/no interrogatives and the structure of responding. *American Sociological Review* 68(6): 939-967.

Sacks, Harvey 1984a. *Lecture 5*, Spring 1972. In Jefferson, G. (ed.), Oxford: Blackwell.

Shuy, Roger W. 1997. Ten unanswered questions about Miranda. *Forensic Linguistics: The International Journal of Speech, Language and the Law* 4(2): 175-196.

CHAPTER EIGHT

A RESPECTED NEUTRAL EXPERT: ARBITRATOR PROFILE IN FOCUS

TARJA SALMI-TOLONEN

This chapter reviews the arbitrator's construction of identity through narratives. Currently, arbitration has become more and more common as a mechanism for the settling of international commercial disputes. One often-mentioned reason for companies opting for international arbitration in cross-border disputes is that the parties themselves can choose their arbitrators (see Hammes et al. 2005; Mistelis 2006 and 2008). The qualities the companies appreciate in arbitrators are their professional qualifications and their track record as lawyers or arbitrators, expertise and experience in the industry or business where the dispute has arisen, and – more importantly – the personality of the arbitrator (cf. e.g. Inkeroinen 2007: 85). Therefore arbitrators' profiles or identities merit investigation. By looking into arbitrators' interviews, I examine how a sense of self or an identity has been conveyed and is indexed and attempt to see whether a common arbitrator profile emerges.

Introduction

In recent years, we have witnessed the decentralisation of the concept of law where law is no longer understood as a body of rules made by the national legislator just as the adjudication process is not solely the concern of public courts. This polycentric view of law includes a new body of rules, practices and processes by private actors, either exercising autonomous regulatory power or implementing delegated power conferred by international law or national legislation (see e.g. Cafaggi 2009 and 2011).

Along with this development, judicial practice has also diversified in nature: private mechanisms of dispute resolution have been established.

International commercial arbitration is an alternative system to national jurisdiction in which the states, their coercive judicial measures and public judicial practices are considered the default. From this point of view arbitration, and other alternative dispute resolution practices, entail the privatisation of public practices and transferring legal practice – conflict resolution – to private commercial actors. International commercial arbitration is one of these private practices for the settling of commercial cross-border disputes and thus exercising delegated power (Salmi-Tolonen 2011).

The language of judicial practice and judges has been studied particularly in the Common Law countries since the 1980s by Danet (1980), Conley / O'Barr (1990), Levi / Walker (1990), Solan (1993), and Maley (1995), to name but a few, but also by Adelswärd et al. (1988) in Sweden. The language of arbitration has not been in the focus of interest, which is probably a natural consequence of the private and confidential nature of arbitration procedure. Nevertheless, Bruce Fraser's paper delivered at the 33rd Annual Conference of the National Academy of Arbitrators entitled "The role of language in arbitration" (Fraser 1980), proves that there has been some interest among the arbitration community. To my understanding, arbitration discourse was not studied in depth or systematically before *the International Commercial Arbitration Practices* research project led by Professor Vijay K. Bhatia.[1] As an international associate to that project I collected data and reported analyses in several research papers but the data contained further aspects to investigate: the arbitrator's identity, which to my knowledge has not been studied before, was one of the traits that emerged even though I had not anticipated it. Arbitrators wear many hats and that is probably one of the reasons why this particular "hat" has not been previously studied.

Material and Methods

We usually think of professional groups in terms of who they are and what they do, but what is professionally achieved is also linguistically achieved and the identities that emerge in daily work are as much linguistic as professional (Richards 2006: 53). The nature and qualifications of arbitration as an institution make the investigation of arbitrators' profiles different from the investigation of other professional identities. For one thing, there is no uniform training for arbitrators, and secondly there is no "workplace" where one could observe arbitrators'

[1] An RGC funded CERG Project No. 9041191: CityU 1501/06H.

interaction to see how group identity is formed, nor is there any knowledge on how large the population of arbitrators who get most of their income from acting as arbitrators actually is. We do have some statistics, such as from Sweden, but they only tell the absolute number of arbitrators (100) and not the number of arbitrators in relation to yearly arbitration procedures. If the number of arbitration procedure is 500-600, it means five cases per arbitrator annually, which would mean full time occupation. This can hardly be the reality because the cases referred to arbitration do not come in a steady flow. In 2011, the Arbitration Institute of the Finland Central Chamber of Commerce released statistics concerning six years from 2006 to 2011, indicating that annually there were 1.2 cases on average per arbitrator. The figures naturally vary from institution to institution (see also Kurkela 2005: 71; Koulu 2008: 494).

In this chapter, I will focus on narrative construction of "the professional arbitrator self" that emerges in the "tellings" of the interviewed arbitrators.[2] One critical question is how far arbitration reality can be reconstructed on the basis of re-contextualised meanings, such as the arbitrator stories. In the present chapter, I will not attempt to answer this question as a whole and to the full but concentrate on arbitrator identity, which for its part is one of the attributes that contribute to the full portrait of international commercial arbitration in real life. Identity here is understood to be in keeping with Krauss (2006: 106) as "processed, socially embedded and readable through the self-stories in which it discursively manifests itself". In order to understand this construction, we therefore need to analyse the telling and the content of such stories.

In order to collect authentic real-life data to compile detailed and "insider" material on arbitration as a mechanism of alternative dispute resolution, experienced arbitrators were interviewed. It seemed also important to discuss arbitration at a more general level with the experts concerning arbitration and face to face with practicing arbitrators. Based on this material and information collected, focused in-depth open-ended interviews with the key actors in arbitration proceedings were conducted.

One of the hypotheses was that although arbitration proceedings are controlled by rules and regulations, in actual practice the knowledge of the arbitration reality and practice resides with the practicing arbitrator/s and counsels representing the parties. Therefore, the purpose was and is to interview several individuals who are in some capacity involved in

---

[2] In this paper, "arbitrator profile" is used to refer to the construction of a collective concept of professional identification, whereas in the course of analysis when referring to individual qualifications, "arbitrator's or arbitrators' profile" will be used.

arbitration procedures. The collected data is secondary material and not primary, collected, for instance, at the arbitration pleadings. Thus, they are also one step removed from the specific discursive context where the talks would naturally occur: in other words, they are re-contextualised.

Re-contextualisation refers to a process which, in brief, concerns transferring and transforming meanings or elements of text from their original context to another (Linell 1998: 154). The process implies changes in the communicative purpose. As a rule, narratives are gathered through interviewing, which is "understood as a discursive act where meaning is negotiated through language" (Alvarez / Urla 2002: 20).

The stories of arbitration, arbitration procedures and arbitrators are in relation to other texts and discourses within the same genre chain as arbitral awards, claimants' and respondents' memoranda, pleadings and counsels' speeches and argumentation, and arbitration laws that have a shared principal purpose or hyper-function, namely to help solve disputes legally. Although each of these sub-genres has its own particular text function, the texts nevertheless have the same overriding purpose. Consequently, the type of re-contextualisation is intertextual or interdiscursive.

The chosen research method means that interviews are treated not only as a source of information but also as research material. All the interviews were recorded to ensure the accuracy of study. The interviews were open-ended for acquiring all relevant information the experts could submit and, in addition, to avoid contaminating the evidence by imposing even unintentionally the interviewee's accounts with the researcher's own presuppositions. This was considered the best procedure as the ground approached is rather uncharted (Salmi-Tolonen 2008a, 2008b and 2009).

The Interviewees and interview settings

For the first stage, three arbitrators who all had several years' experience in US or cross-border arbitration were interviewed. Time spent with one interviewee varied from one and a half hours to two hours. One of the interviews was conducted in London in 2007 and the other two in Finland in 2008 and 2009.

The first interview conducted was with an American emeritus professor of law who has had extensive experience in arbitrating consumer cases especially related to health care in the United States. Apart from being an arbitrator and academic he has also acted as a litigator.

The second interview was conducted with a Finnish arbitrator who has a degree in law and has been trained on the bench and who does not litigate but is employed by consulting businesses in contracting. The cases where she acts as an arbitrator are generally cross-border company disputes.

The third interview was with an emeritus judge of the Finnish Supreme Court who is also a very experienced international arbitrator and active in many domestic and international bodies concerning arbitration, among them the UNCITRAL.

The interviewees were selected rather at random at this stage in the sense that the author knew them personally and professionally and they were willing to recount their experiences and were available without any further travel or other arrangements. In other words, this data gathering phase fulfilled the accessibility criteria.

Focused and open interviews

The interviews were first of all planned to collect arbitrator stories for the purposes of the Arbitration Discourse Project (see *para* footnote 1) to extract important information on arbitration reality. It soon became obvious that narrative analysis could yield interesting information on arbitrator personalities. Therefore, I was interested to see whether the narratives would render certain profiles or a profile that would complement the expectations of the parties or firms that have included arbitration clauses in their contracts. The interviews conducted were focused but open discussions to enable the interviewees to narrate freely their experiences as arbitrator's and describe or reveal something of their identities as arbitrators.

The interviews I personally conducted with practising arbitrators were later complemented by 14 transcriptions of interviews conducted by the City University of Hong Kong team in Hong Kong with eight arbitrators and six lawyers/legal counsels. These interviews were structured and therefore do not contain narrative to the same extent as the open interviews but are, however, useful in order to focus and corroborate the profiles extracted from them. I am very grateful to Professor Bhatia for allowing me to use this source material as well. It is quite clear even now that those interviews are very rich in various kinds of data and merit more investigation beyond this brief discussion.

The face-to-face interviews were focused interviews where the themes were prepared beforehand but they were not structured or even semi-structured in format. Some parts of the interviews were open in that the interviewees recounted their own experiences or reviewed or evaluated the arbitration practices at their own choice. My starting point was that the locus of the epistemic knowledge of the arbitration process was with the interviewees. The interviews collected in Hong Kong were structured, based on questions and answers, and are used to check the observations made of the narrative accounts of experiences of the interviewees. They thus increase the reliability of the results and sharpen the view to the profiles.

The interviews in London and Finland were conducted face to face with the interviewee and the researcher (the author) present. The interviews were recorded and the recordings transcribed later on. I also took notes during the interview. The interviews in Hong Kong were conducted with two or three researchers present, recorded and transcribed. I had the transcriptions at my disposal.

The beginning of the face to face interview as a whole could be described as narrative (here referring to the text type) as I simply asked the interviewees to recount freely their own background, career and experiences before and after being first appointed as an arbitrator. After this narrative the themes discussed were planned beforehand to some extent. This was also to help find out how the interviewees constructed their identities in the arbitration process.

As a rule the interview was conducted fairly freely so that the persons interviewed, if they so wished, talked most of the time and when issues of particular interest came up the researcher would ask additional questions so that the interviewee could elaborate on that theme. Open interviews were considered suitable also because the assumption was that in real-life arbitration there would be lots of practices and issues that were previously unexplored and I did want those to come up spontaneously without the researcher's intervention.

Interview Themes

The themes prepared beforehand are naturally bound to the three issues that came up on the presumptions and hypotheses of the *Arbitration Discourse* project.

Theme I
Interviewee focused data:
Personal account of the interviewee's curriculum on the interviewee's choice (typically: training, type of employments, time) how they became arbitrators, experience and role in arbitration.

Theme II
Task-specific data and the interviewee's role in arbitration proceedings (sole arbitrator, chair of the tribunal, member of a panel)

Theme III
Arbitration proceedings
Personal accounts of one case or a typical case of interviewee's choice

Theme IV
Interviewee as an arbitrator

Theme V
Arbitration parties, outcome, awards, challenges etc. (how, when, who)

Theme VI
Assessment of arbitration as a method of ADR (in comparison with litigation, mediation, conciliation on interviewee's choice)

As already mentioned, the interview flowed very much on the interviewee's terms in order to get a spontaneous account.

Appropriation of narrative analysis

Without going into the discussion of narrative analysis as a method since the analysis does not fit into the influential Labovian model (Labov: 1972) or into an orthodox narrative analysis conception or methodology, the study does not identify itself as belonging to "small stories" but rather several approaches are used eclectically. I should just say that I am in accordance with those views that emphasise strongly "the situated and contextual nature of narrating as activities that are functionally embedded in sociocultural practices" (Bamberg 2006: 141). It is within these practices that they become interpretable and analysable for what they are accomplishing. One part of the activities is that they also index who is speaking/writing, from which position, and for what purpose. In short, narratives cannot be taken simply and interpreted solely for what has been said and told. Rather, they have to be analysed, and the analysis of narratives has to work with what we have, the actual wording and the delivery/style of the wording. "The analysis has to work through this in order to perceive how a sense of self – or an identity – has been conveyed and is indexed" (Bamberg 2006: 141). Of particular interest are the pragmatics of the stories; how the interviewees renegotiate the context and their professional identity and what the open and covert recontextualisation cues used are.

Linell (1998: 144-145) describes re-contextualisation as the "dynamic transfer- and -transformation of something from one discourse / text in context to another" which involves "the extrication of some part or aspect from a text or discourse or from a genre of texts or discourses, and fitting of this part or aspect into another context and its use and environment". We can also speak about genre embedding here in Bhatia's (2004: 186) terms because these interviews can be described as a particular generic form which is used as a template to give expression to another conventionally distinct generic form. In Figure 8-1 I try to illustrate the relationship between the context of arbitration and the two re-contextualisations of it.

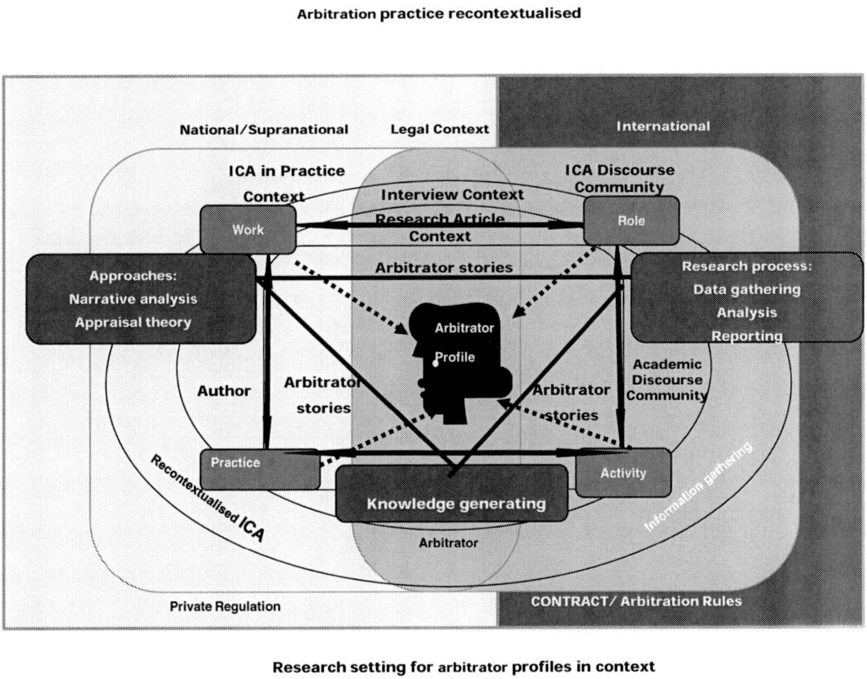

Figure 8-1 Research setting for arbitrator profiles in context

International commercial arbitration is inseparably embedded in global and national legal environments. Arbitration practice puts these legal norms into action. Every facet of arbitration reality hinges on contextual factors. Figure 8-1 depicts first of all the various contexts involved: the rules and regulations, both public and private, that regulate arbitration and enable it to function as a dispute resolution mechanism. The outer sphere represents the legal context and environment: public regulation and legal principles; domestic (Arbitration Acts), international (e.g. UNCITRAL

Model Law) and supranational enabling freedom to contract; private regulation e.g. arbitration rules of arbitration institutes, contracts that lay down the rules for the contracting parties and arbitration clauses. The next context is international commercial arbitration practice and the discourse community of various actors in arbitration reconstructed in the interviews in the form of arbitrator narratives. The interview also constitutes a particular kind of context with a particular kind of information and data-gathering purpose where arbitration practice is re-contextualised in interaction with the interviewer and the interviewee – the researcher and the arbitrator. The interview context is inevitably structured by academic research principles and practices. Its aim is to collect research data to be analysed and studied according to contested research methods to produce findings. The findings will then be reported in a research article or other academic publication complying with the convention of the academic scientific discourse community. The corners of the triangle represent the approaches and analyses methods chosen in order to generate new knowledge. To get a focused picture of the arbitrator profile four parameters are used: role, practice, activity and work represented by the four corners of the square encircling the profile in the middle. All these contribute to the formation of arbitrator profiles and will be explained in detail below.

There is plenty of meaning going around in stories and it is valuable in showing how identity gets renegotiated and reconstructed in and through interaction. I am in accordance with Freeman (2006: 132) in that "narrative thus gets taken down to size".

In Table 8-1 below, a structural model of the arbitrators' tale is presented. It is clear that this table only indicates the small data collected so far, but in some ways the tellings were so similar that it seems reasonable to assume that there will only be variations in details.

All the arbitrators I personally interviewed said that they were not full-time arbitrators but had other posts. The arbitrators in this project represent different kinds of legal professions: academic, private entrepreneur, judge. I took this to provide a backdrop and highlight the shared properties, on the one hand, and individual variation, on the other. The interviews were collected within the framework of a research project led by Professor Vijay K. Bhatia[3], who involved researchers and teams in more than 20 jurisdictions all over the world (see Bhatia et al. 2003).

---

[3] See *para* note 1.

Role in the narrative	Narrative focus	Propositional content	Stance marker	Stance
Introducing the narrator	Arbitrator focus	professional career arbitration career facts of lived life	I cannot remember I never sought I was invited	non-ambitious innocent but not naive by chance
Setting the arbitration scene	Task focus	Factual context of cases - institutional - ad hoc	an enjoyable process	approval / highly positive / no conflict of roles
Reciting the procedure	Administrative phase Preliminary hearing Evidentiary hearing Issuing the award	Observations - more informal (than litigation) - final, enforceable	- their performance is better - more flexible - you just sit there and relax and answer the questions - less disruptive	proactive cooperative

Table 8-1 The structure of the arbitrator's tale

Arbitrator's profiles

The hypothesis was that the interviews would describe and reveal something of the interviewees' identities as arbitrators. Thus, the interviews were treated not only as a source of information but also as material for profiling and analysis. Arbitrator interviewees are analysed in respect of four aspects in a model adapted from a five dimensional model for understanding professional identity in information architecture: title, practice, activity, thing (Hinton 2008).

By looking into arbitrator interviews, I try to perceive how a sense of self or an identity has been conveyed and indexed (see Bamberg 2006: 141). As has been pointed out by Rosenholz (1989: 125, 162) that "A story is constitutive; it makes for collective identification".

It is generally assumed that groups develop characteristic ways of speaking and acting which are achieved *through* discourse not merely *in* it. In this study, cognitive entities, traditionally treated as analytic resources, are approached empirically as participants' ways of talking. This naturally leads to an interest in aspects of discourse construction, both in terms of its features (stories, metaphors, accounts, etc.) and in terms of the way it constructs versions of the world (Bamberg 2006: 52): in this case, the lives lived and the world of conflict resolution.

As was pointed out at the outset, if there is "an arbitrator group identity" it cannot be studied by observing the group interacting. Also to avoid the dangers of home-spun psychology or basing the assumptions on the fact that the interviewees are practising arbitrators and therefore belong to this "group", I decided to look into the interviewees' talk in connection with four aspects inspired by Andrew Hinton's model for understanding professional identity (Hinton 2008). The parameters in this study are: practice, role, activity, and work. These aspects together form the content of what the term "arbitrator" denotes.

	ICA AS	**ACTIVITY**	
Practice	***Role***	***Activity***	***Work***
Shared history of learning	Hat	The actual work of conducting the activity	The activity itself
Legal education Arbitrator training	For the person performing	Organising	Dispute
Tacit knowledge	Conflict solving	Dispute resolution	Means to reach a solution
Experience	Arbitrator	Arbitration	Arbitral award

Table 8-2 International Commercial Arbitration as Activity

To make Table 8-2 understandable, I will explain the parameters which have commonplace and self-explanatory denominators below. The first column "Practice" emerges from a community that coalesces around a shared concern and which affiliates strongly with the role over time. Parties choose arbitrators on the basis of the following parameters: general qualifications for acting as arbitrator and neutral, professional qualifications and experience as lawyer, experience as arbitrator, experience and expertise in the industry or business in question, the personality of the actor, a good manager or organiser.

The second column "Role" describes the "Hat" the person is wearing. Generally speaking, the roles may change and the same person is not a full-time arbitrator but can also be a litigator or a legal counsel or head of a legal department, etc. In this case, the hat is the arbitrator's figurative hat. The hat symbolises an arbitrator, legal counsel representing the parties, single arbitrator, a chair of the tribunal or one of the members of the tribunal.

"Activity" refers to the actual work the person does in the literal act of working to solve conflicts and disputes. The activity then is arbitration, its procedural organisation and the material procedure.

"Work" is the issue the person is working with. In this case, the issue is a breach of contract, the details causes of the conflict, and the means to solve it. Work here refers to the arbitral procedure which ends in an arbitral award/decision which is legal, enforceable, and non-public. The procedure must be based on principles of equity or fairness, and must not be in conflict with the principles of *ordre public*, due process or natural justice.

Now that we have established the setting, we can look into the types of expressions studied in pursuit of the arbitrator identity.

Expressions of appraisal

The linguistic features I looked into recall those also known in Appraisal Theory developed by Martin / White (2007), which they explain to be an extension to the interpersonal meta-function described in the framework of M.A.K. Halliday and his colleagues' as Systemic Functional Linguistics (see e.g. Halliday 2004; Martin 1992, Mattiessen 1995). As narrative performance refers to "a site of struggle over personal, social and professional identity rather than a fixed essence", the expressions of appraisal seem particularly suited for analysis to extract both the personal and professional self of the interviewed arbitrators (see Langellier 2001: 151). Appraisal theory is concerned with those meanings which vary the terms of the speaker's engagement with their utterances, which vary what is at stake interpersonally both in individual utterances and as the texts unfolds cumulatively (Martin / White 2007: 6). The following are in accordance with the appraisal theory's subtypes of appraisal. The expressions identified in each subtype are from the present data.

a) Attitude:

Values by which speakers pass judgement and associate emotional/affectual responses with participants and processes (http://grammatics.com/appraisal/).

Attitude includes those meanings by which speakers attach an intersubjective value or assessment to participants and processes by reference either to emotional responses or to systems of culturally-determined value systems. The appraisal theorists have divided attitude into three sub-systems:

- Affect: the characterisation of phenomena by reference to emotion
- Judgement: the evaluation of human behaviour with respect to social norms
- Appreciation: the evaluation of objects and products (rather than human behaviour) by reference to aesthetic principles and other systems of social value. (http://grammatics.com/appraisal/)

In my data I found the following types of expressions of attitude towards the parties:

Use of pronoun or always third person *I*/*we*/third person
Verbs used to *tell*, *ask* as an imperative (modality)

A: I tell them that I will not tolerate ... I/them; tell (command)
B: We can find a solution to this together. We
C: If the parties are in agreement, I will ask the counsels ... Third person; ask (command)

Arbitrator A's narrative is in the first person and A is very much present in the telling. The attitude towards the parties can be described as authoritative in a way you generally associate with, say, a father of a family, a teacher at school or a baseball or football coach in a minor league. Arbitrator B again sees the arbitral procedure as a common effort, between both the arbitrator and the parties: we will manage this together. A style associated with many counselling (family counselling or health counselling) situations and similar expressions are also used in kindergarten and other nursing contexts.[4] Arbitrator C uses a hedged expression as a commanding verb, namely *ask* rather than *tell*. I interpret this to show more distance between the arbitrator and the parties.

[4] In the US, Professor Susan Daicoff has coined a term referring to a movement that utilises the insight of procedural justice and other social science-based understanding of the interpersonal dynamics of legal disputes and legal affairs. Problem-solving courts in the US are examples of the comprehensive law movement.

b) Engagement:

Resources for positioning the speaker's/author's voice with respect to the various propositions and proposals conveyed by a text; meanings by which speakers either acknowledge or ignore the diversity of viewpoints put at risk by their utterances and negotiate an interpersonal space for their own positions within that diversity. The meanings analysed under engagement are typically analysed in the literature under the various headings of evidentiality, epistemic modality and hedging – lexico-grammatical resources such as modals of probability (*it seems, apparently*), projection/attribution, hearsay and so on (http://grammatics.com/appraisal/).

Modal expressions:

A: I don't really remember. It is an enjoyable process for a number of reasons.
B: It was a surprise, I became arbitrator by accident.
proclamation, counter-expectation
B: My way of doing this… Proactive help companies avoid conflicts I hope I can help them help themselves
expectation

All the arbitrators I personally interviewed had become arbitrators more or less by chance, they had not set becoming an arbitrator as their objective but had been asked to perform. Chance is perhaps not the right word because their training and activities in working life were closely connected with various kinds of conflicts. In arbitrator B's story the help aspect comes up again.

c) Graduation:

In appraisal theory, graduation refers to values by which speakers graduate, raise or lower the interpersonal impact, force or volume of their utterances by which they graduate (blur or sharpen) the focus of their semantic categorisations (http://grammatics.com/appraisal/).

- usually
- very different
- it is hard to say
- more relaxed
- roughly the same
- quite lenient

The data was then analysed based on these expressions within the appraisal theoretical parameters which, in turn, were posited into the action theoretical framework. On the basis of the analyses, the interviewees were then considered as possessing three distinct profiles, which will be explained below in the next section. The research setting of arbitrator profiles is described in Figure 8-1 above.

Arbitrator profiles

On the basis of the analysis of these attributes three different types of profiles were drafted: a Coach, a Healer and an Administrator.

The qualifications of these three profiles fall into the attributes described above: practice, role, activity and work are listed in Table 8-3 below.

	A	B	C
PRACTICE	law degree university not planned	law degree private practice by accident	law degree court always interested
ROLE	Coach	Healer	Administrator
ACTIVITY	solve disputes telling the parties how "them"	solve disputes by helping the parties help themselves "us"	sole disputes with parties "by the book" "party" "parties" 3rd person
WORK	Enthusiasm	Satisfaction	Content

Table 8-3 Three arbitrator profiles

Table 8-3 shows us that both shared and individual qualities can be found in the profiles. The shared qualities are collected into Table 8-4 below.

The shared qualities fall into the attributes of practice, activity and work as, of course, were expected. The individual qualities, again, are most prominent and obvious in the role or the hat slot. Table 8-5 below shows how the attributes of appraisal theory are expressed and distributed between the discerned roles.

PRACTICE	Legal qualifications, law degree, LL.M. – LL.D. qualifications to litigate, trained on the bench Double qualifications: surveying, construction, engineering Professional experience: in industry, at the bar, on the bench, academia Entering arbitration practice: was asked to, by chance
ACTIVITY	My way, this is how I usually do it, conversational, less intimidating than court
WORK	Enthusiasm, worthwhile

Table 8-4 Shared qualities

HAT	COACH: I tell them that I will not tolerate ... I/them; tell (command) HEALER: We can find a solution to this together. I try to help them help themselves. ADMINISTRATOR: If the parties are in agreement, I will ask the counsels … Third person; ask (command)	ATTITUDES VALUES ENGAGEMENT GRADUATION

Table 8-5 Individual qualities

The second set of interviews, the Hong Kong interviews, rendered direct information in response to a direct question on the qualifications the interviewees would be looking for when choosing an arbitrator to solve their dispute. The 14 interviews conducted by the Hong Kong team corroborate, at least, the findings of profiles A and C. Such background variables as gender, training and legal system may have had some influence on the opinions. It is hard to say whether this was because of the fact that all the 14 either arbitrators, counsels or stakeholders were male or that many of them knew the common law legal context better. One expression that came up several times when the interviewees were asked about the grounds for their choice of arbitrator was that "we want a good pair of hands" or "we want someone who can manage our case" or "a good organiser". These would fall into the category of "affect" and "judgement" in appraisal theory terms. Therefore, we can conclude that this information corroborates particularly the first and third profiles: an authority who manages the case for the parties in conflict.

Conclusions

In every research process based on real data, there comes a stage when you have collected your data, rich in information directly relevant to your current research hypothesis and questions, but also rich in other information that you did not know existed or were not looking for. This piece of research is a case in point. I was collecting data for the arbitration in action project to learn about arbitration as a dispute resolution mechanism, but in addition to that, it turned out that the data also consisted of material on the arbitrators themselves, both as personalities and as arbitrator types. The purpose of this study was to see if common or shared personal qualifications of arbitrators could be established to reveal a common identity of arbitrators, or what their fundamental assumptions and concerns are and what vocabularies they used in their tales and whether their usual way of interacting would be found. This was considered important since what the parties/companies experiencing cross-border commercial disputes have reported is they appreciate certain types of personal qualities of an arbitrator they would like to handle their case (Hammes 200; Mistelis 2006, 2008).

Information and data-gathering was carried out by open thematic interviews with experienced arbitrators. The interview data were not treated only as a source of information but also as research data as such. The data were analysed with eclectic methods combining narrative analysis, re-contextualisation theory and appropriation theory. The model with four attributes of professional identity was appropriated from a model which Hinton (2008) proposed in order to understand professional identity and practice in information architecture: practice, role, activity, and work. The findings rendered both shared and individual qualifications as follows.

To conclude, then, what connects at least the interviewed practicing arbitrators are:

Shared:
Practice: Legal qualifications, law degree: (LL.M.-LL.D; qualifications to litigate, trained on the bench)
Professional experience: in industry, courts, universities
Entering arbitration practice: by chance, was asked
Work: Enthusiasm, worthwhile
Action: My way, this is how I usually do it, conversational, less intimidating than court

Individual:
Hat: Authority, Healer, Administrator

The findings thus indicate that at least based on this selection of data an arbitrator profile can be discerned and in addition some particular types of arbitrators. However, a wider collection of narratives may add new types. One of the factors that might have made the results somewhat skewed is the representations of gender – only one of the interviewees was female. Arbitrators are predominantly male but so far there is no contested evidence on how the professional profiles of female and male might differ in respects studied in this paper.

According to this analysis, there appears to be a professional arbitrator profile characterised by good managerial and organisational skills but also there is room for individuality. One could conclude that while it is important for aspiring arbitrators to show their professional membership by no means should they need to leave their individual mentalities at the door of the arbitration tribunal.

Although this investigation has in no way solved the mysteries of identity or personality of experienced arbitrators, I hope I have been able to locate some interesting coordinates in the world of arbitration. Research papers must end but research goes on. There are still many unexplored areas in arbitration – among others the attitudes of common law and civil law arbitrators and counsels in arbitration and their comparison. The data gathered already provide material for such an investigation.

References

Adelswärd, Viveka / Aronsson, Karin / Linell, Per 1988. Discourse of blame: courtroom constructions of social identity from the perspective of the defendant. *Semiotica* 71: 261-284.

Alvarez, Rosario / Urla, Jaqueline 2002. Tell me a good story: using narrative analysis to examine information requirements interviews during the ERP implementation. *The Database for Advancement in Information Systems* 33(1): 38-52.

Appraisal theory <http://grammatics.com/appraisal/:>.

Bamberg, Michael 2006. Stories: big or small. Why do we care? *Narrative Inquiry* 16 (1): 139-147.

Bhatia, Vijay K. / Candlin, Christopher N. / Engberg, Jan / Trosborg, Anna 2003. *Multilingual and Multicultural Contexts of Legislation: An International Perspective.* Frankfurt am Main: Peter Lang.

Bhatia, Vijay K. 2004. *Worlds of Written Discourse: A Genre-based View.* London: Continuum.

Cafaggi, Fabrizio 2009. Private regulation in European Private Law, EUI Working Papers, *RSCAS* 2009/31, Florence: 1-32

—. 2011. New foundations of transnational private regulation, *Journal of Law and Society* 38(1): 20-49.

Conley, John M. / O'Barr, Michael, 1990. *Rules Versus Relationships: The Ethnography of Legal Discourse.* Chicago: The University of Chicago Press.

Danet, Brenda 1980. Language in the legal process. *Law And Society Review* 14: 445-564.

Fraser, Bruce 1980. The role of language in arbitration. In *Proceedings of the 33rd Annual Meeting of the National Academy of Arbitrators.* Available at http://www.naarb.org/proceedings/pdfs/1980-19.pdf: 19-44.

Freeman, Mark 2006. Life "on holiday"? In defense of big stories. *Narrative Inquiry* 16: 131-138.

Hammes, Michael et al. 2005. Commercial Dispute Resolution – a comparative study of resolution procedures in Germany. PriceWaterhouseCoopers. Available at www.pwc.com/Extweb/pwcpublications.

Halliday, Michael A.K. 2004/1994. *An Introduction to Functional Grammar*. London: Edward Arnold.

Hinton, Andrew 2008. A model for understanding professional identity and practice. A closing talk at the IA Summit in Miami, FL, April 14, 2008. Available at http://www.inkblurt.com/2008/05/07/a-model-for-understanding-professional-identity-and-practice/.

Inkeroinen, Pekka 2007. Kansainvälinen välimiesmenettely erityistapauksena. (International arbitration as a case in point tr. TST) In Turunen S. (ed.) *Välimiesmenettely lainkäyttönä ja lainkäytössä*. (Arbitration in legal practice and as legal practice) Conflict Management. Helsinki: Edita, 77-105.

Koulu, Risto 2008. Kuka kaipaa välimiesmenettelyä? (Who would need arbitration? tr. TST) *Oikeus* 2008 37(4): 494-503.

Krauss, Wolfgang 2006. The narrative negotiation of identity and belonging. *Narrative Inquiry* 16 (1): 103-111.

Kurkela, Matti S. 2005. *Due Process in International Commercial Arbitration.* New York: Oceana Publications.

Labov, William 1972. The transformation of reality in narrative syntax. In Labov, W. *Language in the Inner City*. Philadelphia: University of Philadelphia Press: 354-396.

Langellier, Kristin M. 2001. "You are marked": Breast cancer, tattoo, and the narrative performance of identity. In Brockmayer, J. and Carbaugh, D. (eds) *Narrative and Identity. Studies in Autobiography, Self and Culture*. Amsterdam: John Benjamins. 145-184.

Levi, Judith / Walker, Graffam A. 1990. *Language in the Judicial Process 3*. New York: Plenum Press.
Linell, Per 1998. *Approaching Dialogue*. Amsterdam: John Benjamins.
Maley, Yon 1995. From adjudication to mediation: third party discourse in conflict resolution. *Journal of Pragmatics* 23 (1): 93-110.
Martin, James R. 1992. *English Text: System and Structure*. Amsterdam: John Benjamins.
Martin, James R. / White, Peter R.R. 2007. *Language of Evaluation: Appraisal in English*. Basingstoke: Palgrave Macmillan.
Matthiessen C 1995. *Lexicogrammatical Cartography: English Systems*. Tokyo: International Language Science Publishers.
Mistelis, Loukas 2006. The study: perceptions tested – myths, data and analysis. International arbitration: corporate attitudes and practices. PriceWaterhouseCoopers. Available at http://www.pwc.be/en_BE/be/publications/ia-study-pwc-06.pdf.
—. 2008 International arbitration: corporate attitudes and practices. Available at http://www.pwc.co.uk/en_UK/uk/assets/pdf/pwc-international-arbitration-2008.pdf.
Richards, Keith 2006. *Language and Professional Identity. Aspects of Collaborative Interaction*. New York: Palgrave Macmillan.
Rosenholz, Susan J. 1989. *Teachers' Workplace: The Social Organization of Schools.* London: Longman.
Salmi-Tolonen, Tarja 2008a. The Arbitrator's Tale. A paper read at an International Conference Curriculum, Language and the Law, Dubrovnik, September 18-21, 2008.
—. 2008b. Stance and emergent identity in arbitrators' stories. A paper read at an International Workshop: *Linguistic and Discursive Aspects or International Arbitration*. University of Milan, September 22-13, 2008.
—. 2009. Arbitrator profile revisited. A paper read at a Panel: *Exploring Discourses and Practices of International Commercial Arbitration*. LSP 2009, University of Aarhus, August 17-21, 2009.
—. 2011, Introduction. In Salmi-Tolonen, T. / Tukiainen, I. / Foley, R. (eds.) *Law and Language in Partnership and Conflict. A Special Issue of the Lapland Law Review* 1 (1). Available at http://www.ulapland.fi/LaplandLawReview: 1-13.
Solan, Lawrence M. 1993. *The Language of Judges*. Chicago: The University of Chicago Press.

CHAPTER NINE

ROLE HYBRIDITY IN PROFESSIONAL PRACTICE IN A HEARING IN THE SPECIAL CRIMINAL COURT

VIEIRA TORRES AMITZA

Introduction

Hybridity can be considered a pervasive phenomenon that takes place in all the spheres of contemporary society. In a historical context, when there is an ongoing contact among different groups, cultural hybridity has represented a social and historical phenomenon since early human migration. The notion of hybridity can also be applied in other areas such as biology, agronomy, mechanics, etc. In language studies for instance this concept means word formation by subsequent addition of roots from different languages.

In the area of linguistic studies, hybridity and hybridisation are not simply linguistic processes manifest through intertextuality and interdisursivity. Following Sarangi / Roberts (1999), discourse hybridity or hybrid forms of speech include multiple shifts in modality related to levels of identity, forms of speech, socialisation in communities of practice, *backstage / frontstage* negotiation, and so on. Extending this notion in a recent work, Sarangi (2011) defines role hybridity as the co-existence in professional contexts, in different ways (of genres, voices, activities) marked by creation and purpose. According to the author, hybridity and hybridisation "constitute communicative acts mediated by role-relationships in context-sensitive ways" (2011: 272). Therefore Sarangi (2011) proposes extending the notion of hybridity to the role *performance* (Goffman [1959] 1985) in professional contexts.

In this discussion, concepts such as self, identity, status and role are central to our analytical endeavours. However, these concepts are used interchangeably, and sometimes in a conflated manner (e.g. self-identity, role-identity) by scholars within and across different analytical domains with overlapping ontological and epistemological trajectories. Based on ideas from sociological and social psychological traditions, such as the concepts of role (Goffman 1959), role-set (Merton 1968) and character-work (Strong / Davis 1978), Sarangi (2011: 272) suggests that

> the notion of 'role' with all its complexity is perhaps more operationalizable at the social interactional level, and especially in the institutional/professional domains, than the notions of self, identity and status.

Accordingly, this chapter takes the notion of 'role' as an organising concept used on occasion by actors in social settings (Goffman 1959). For Goffman (1961: 87), "it is through roles that tasks in society are allocated and arrangements made to enforce their performance". Based on Sarangi's perspective (2000, 2010, 2011) about discourse hybridity in professional contexts, this study aims to investigate the roles played by a judge in a Hearing of the Special Criminal Court in a city of Zona da Mata, state of Minas Gerais, Brazil. In detail we seek to:

i. describe the roles played by the judge in a hearing in the Special Criminal Court;
ii. investigate the reasons to explain why certain roles are highlighted in this talk-in-interaction;
iii. identify which roles are played of his/her own free will and which are imposed by virtue of the specific institutional mandate in a Criminal Hearing.

The investigation of the performance of professional roles in a legal context may contribute to the study of interactional linguistics, as it brings relevant empirical insights to the theory.

Theoretical Orientation

First of all, based on Sarangi (2010), we will discuss the established distinctions between social role, discourse role and activity role. The first concept explored here refers to the social relationship between the participants in an interaction (mother-child, teacher-student, doctor-patient, judge-defendant, etc.). By discourse role we understand the relationship between the participants and the message (if s/he is producing it, receiving it, transmitting it on behalf of another, etc.). Finally, activity role is dependent on the activity type the individual is participating in and is usually defined in relation to other participants. For instance, a chairperson role is only legitimate in the meeting session in the co-presence of other committee members, assuming there is a prior institutional mandate (Maynard 1984) regarding his/her activity role. Before and after the meeting session and also during the coffee break the activity role of chairperson dissipates and even during the meeting itself such a role may shift as the chairperson articulates his/her views as a committee member rather than as a chairperson (Sarangi 2010).

According to Sarangi (2011), any discussion concerning the notion of role must go back to Ralph Linton ([1945] 1971), who equates social role to status. Linton (1971: 112) considers status "the position of an individual in the prestige system of a society", whereas role designates "the sum total of the culture patterns associated with a particular status". In this way each social status in which people find themselves may involve a different group of roles.

Robert Merton (1968) challenges Linton's view. The author considers role-sets as a middle-range theory to underpin how social status is organised in the social structure. For him, "role-set theory begins with the concept that each social status involves not a single associated role, but an array of roles" (Merton 1968: 42). According to Merton, role-set is that complement of social relationships in which persons are involved simply because they occupy a particular social status. For example, the teacher takes on an array of roles in relation to his/her student (advisor, educator, evaluator), but in relation to other teachers we may find a different array of roles (co-worker, co-author, evaluator) (Sarangi 2011).

For Sarangi (2010), role-set differs from multiple roles. So the author goes back to Merton (1968: 42), who explains that the latter term (multiple roles) has traditionally referred not to the complex of roles associated with a *single* social status but to the various social statuses (often in different institutional spheres) in which people find themselves. Thus, we would find, for example, a woman connected with the distinct statuses of teacher, wife, mother, Catholic, Republican and so on. Merton (1968: 424) designates this complement of social statuses of an individual as his status-set, each of the statuses in turn having its distinctive role-set. For instance the characterisation of the doctor's role can be traced to Foucault (1972), who identifies what can be seen as a role-set that combines aspects of education, therapy, gatekeeping as well as safeguarding the common good (Sarangi 2011: 41).

Following this discussion, Mehan (1986) points out that, in terms of role-set, the classroom teacher may be an authority figure in the classroom, but he occupies a peripheral role-status in the committee meeting (Mehan 1986: 141). Another study to consider is Tannen and

Wallat (2002) who see role-shifting as frame shifts in the context of paediatric interaction – between the interrogative official mode and an informal conversational mode. The doctor seems to shift between her therapeutic role and what can be called a pseudo-parental role. The effortless ways in which the participants negotiate their turns, design their recipients, accompanied by register shifts, suggest that these encounters are characterised by a mutual recognition of hybridised role performance. A further study is provided by Strong and Davis (1978),who suggest that parents have expert and detailed knowledge about their children, so the doctor's scientific and generalised expertise is bound to be contingent on parents' expertise. Also the diffused role-responsibilities of a clergyman – cultural leader, teacher, medical or social worker – can be moved into a central place by the clergyman, eclipsing his specifically religious responsibilities (Elliott 1972: 126).

In the academic sphere, professionals find themselves in competing and conflicting roles when acting out supervisor and assessor responsibilities simultaneously in relation to a student's dissertation/project. While one part of the role-set is meant to be one of facilitating and scaffolding, the other part is one of gatekeeping (Sarangi 2011: 38). However, for Sarangi (2011), the role-sets can be seen as role hybridity not always in conflict, but often in a complementary relation, like the Criminal Hearing we are focusing on here.

On Data and Research Methodology

Generally speaking, research methodology can be classified as qualitative. Qualitative data typically emphasises what is relevant in social life, that is, in a qualitative research the aim is to investigate the quality of social action and meaning. For Levinson (1983), linguistic-discursive patterns, structures and resources are established more in terms of expectations concerning interactional routines rather than statistical approach. And that is the (strategic) use of certain resources – or their (strategic) absence – considering sequences of action that guide the participants to the construction of situated inferences and meanings which are co-constructed and negotiated in the interaction (Silveira 2007).

Following Erickson (1992), researchers must pay attention to what is seen and heard. In a qualitative research method, concepts and theories emerge from the data where we may find examples of the main notions. There is a dynamic interaction between data and theory. Qualitative research, according to the author, seeks to describe the main events that are important and establish a co-relation between these events and the wider social context in order to be used as concrete examples of abstract principles governing social organisation.

The qualitative approach is characterised, therefore, by immersion of the researcher in the context. The search is guided by the interpretation and the researcher can be considered an interpreter of reality. Therefore we analyse the interaction data in real speech, our analysis is guided by our own researcher perception (interpretation) and we regard the possible communicative intent of the speakers in the production of their utterances.

The data in our study were generated in a Hearing of the Special Criminal Court, in a city of Zona da Mata, state of Minas Gerais. In this professional setting the judge orients himself/herself to the accomplishment of an institutional mandate (Maynard 1984), that is, to judge a legal case. This kind of Hearing involves criminal contraventions and misdemeanours (under two years' imprisonment) and macro-structural organisation of the event corresponds to:

- Testimony assessment;
- Investigation of the facts;
- Attempt to reach an agreement between the parties;
- Judgment;
- Passing sentence.

The data in this study belong to the scope of the Project PIBIC/UFJF/2007-2008 "Portuguese spoken in Zona da Mata, state of Minas Gerais, Brazil: database of Preliminary Hearings in the Special Criminal Court". We used a 22min. 34s. audio-recorded encounter in court as the source of our analysis. The examples were selected from the qualitative analysis of the sequential organisation of talk in this institutional context. Transcription conventions follow conversation analysis method (Sacks / Schegloff / Jefferson 1974).

The participants are: the judge, Mary (victim/complainant) and Joseph (defendant). Mary and Joseph are both retired farmers with a low educational level. The Hearing takes place in order to check what was registered in the police report by Mary, who had accused Joseph of threatening her with death. However, during the Hearing, Mary says that Joseph had taken her house close to the coffee plantations and had killed a cow which belonged to Mary. Then the victim changes the subject insisting on facts that were not previously reported, which causes conflict in the interaction between her and the Judge.

Data Analysis

Our analysis identified two interactional role-sets enacted by the Judge in a Hearing of the Special Criminal Court. The first concerns the judge's professional activities in this institutional context: listen to the testimony of the parties and investigate the facts (inquirer); try to reach an agreement (mediator) and give instructions to parties about the legal procedures in that institutional mandate (expert). The second role-set enacted by the Judge assumes a pedagogic character, concerning oriented instructional explanations: advise the defendant on moral values (advisor); instruct the parties in suitable social behaviour during the Hearing (educator); explain to the defendant what must be done to abide by the sentence (information provider) and send the offender to prison (police authority) if necessary.

Professional role-set

At the beginning of the Hearing, the Judge takes on the role of professional inquirer, asking the defendant about the threats against Mary, with the purpose of checking the whole story registered in the police report, as we can see in the excerpt below.

Example (1)

11 12	Judge	what happened to you Joseph and Mary, Joseph? **have you <u>threa↑</u>tened <u>Ma</u>ry, Joe**?
13	Joseph	me?
14	Judge	yeah↑

Shortly after questioning Joseph, the Judge continues to assess the testimonies, leading the victim to describe the content of the threats she had suffered.

Example (2)

40 41	Judge	**Mary, what did he say to you to make you feel threatened?**
42 43	Mary	I don't acce↑pt this! no:o I was looking in the middle of the land the gate to the land ( ) [ ]
44 45	Judge	um hum, **but what was hi:s threat to you?**

46	Mary	don't like ( ) [ ]
47 48 49 50 51	Judge	um hum. that's okay, Mary, I will ask you aga:in, cause you didn't answer me. **how did he threaten you?** did he say: "Mary I will kill you!" or he took a gun pointed it at you

The focus of mediation is to reach an agreement, to overcome the conflict. In other words, we can say the mediator is responsible for making the communication flow between the parties. This role is played by the Judge in the following examples. In example (3), the Judge seeks to convince the defendant to leave the house which represents in fact the core of the conflict; in example (4), the officer in that law court suggests Mary should sell the house to the defendant.

Example (3)

134 135	Mary	that's it. he (could) leave. the guy told him to donate the house ( )
136	Judge	yeah?
137	Mary	yeah. donate the house
138 139	Judge	**that's right? Why don't you leave this place Joe?**
140	Joseph	what?
141	Judge	**why don't you leave this place↑**
142 143	Joseph	°no°. to leave? eh- I have no place to go (.) I bought the house. If she pays me I'll leave.

Example (4)

147 148 149 150	Mary	( ) I take medication for depression and the doctor said that if I remain there I'll have to take medication for depression forever and I'm so sick and tired.
151	Judge	**why don't you sell it to him?**
152	Mary	Jesus Chri:↑st!

In example (5), the Judge talks about the kind of case that is being conducted and proposes the criminal transaction, taking on the role of expert, someone with detailed knowledge of legal field.

Example (5)

Judge	Joe, listen up: **this case here is a criminal case, okay?** that she moved against you alleging that you would have threatened her of death. all right? you are a first-time offender. **being a first-time offender you have the right, the benefit called criminal transaction, okay? what does this benefit mean? that's an opportunity that is given to the defendant in case of being a first-time offender, not to respond to legal process okay? then you would have to pay a fine that is a minimum wage, and I will send it to a non-profit organisation that is registered here. then you wouldn't have to respond to this process, okay?**

Pedagogic role-set

In example (6), it seems the Judge goes beyond her role as advisor in the Hearing by showing the defendant's moral rules that govern a society and must not be broken.

Example (6)

Joseph	I consider her as my mother, that's her who is (judging) me
Judge	but, if you consider her as a mother, and you say you'll kill her? oh! **but a son never kills her mother, doesn't he?**
	yeah uh hh

In the following excerpts, the role of the Judge is that of an educator, enhanced by the way certain behaviour rules are expressed in that institutional event: the use of intensifiers to express emphasis, the selection of certain forms to show the speaker's feelings of dislike or annoyance as well as the rising intonation given which reminds us the pedagogic setting of a classroom ("QUI:iet down", "little chai::r").

Example (7)

3	Judge	an::d >let me talk< what's your name again?
4	Mary	Mary of ( ) [ ]
5 6	Judge	**Ma:ary, you mus:n't TALk, okay? QUI:iet down!**
7	Mary	okay.
8	Judge	all ri↑ght?

Example (8)

74 75 76	Judge	all right. **no↑w you go sit there on your little chai::r, qui::et down cause now I'll talk to him. okay?**
77	Mary	Okay
78 79	Judge	**then, you won't say a word. he let you talk all right?**
80	Mary	°all right°
81	Judge	now I'll talk to Joe. okay?
82	Mary	okay.

Although explaining the steps to pass sentence represents one of the Judge's functions in this Hearing the Judge seemingly moves beyond this role to provide detailed information about what Joseph should do to serve the sentence. We shall draw on the next excerpts to illustrate this role of information provider.

Example (9)

158 159 160 161 162 163 164	Judge	no, you can pay it. but you have to bring me the receipt to attach to the process. **do you know that piece of papel that you get there in the bank? when you make a deposit? then the cashier gives it to us, as a proof that you made the deposit? that piece of paper has to be attached here to the case.**
165	Joseph	and do I bring them all at once?
166	Judge	the best is to bring them one by one.

Example (10)

251 252 253 254 255 256 257	Judge	you'll have to pay two hundred seven reais all ri↑ght? can you see it here? you can pay it until the 27th. **you'll make a deposit in this bank, Bank of Brazil. when you make the deposit there, you'll bring this paper here and attach this case here look. you'll go to the Bank and show this. you'll come to the reception area.**
258	Joseph	here?
259 260 261	Judge	**here in lawcourt. do you know that office downstairs where you read Reception? do you know which one? did you understand?**
262	Joseph	um hum
263	Judge	then God bless you

The role of police authority includes arresting the offender. In this Hearing, the Judge enacts this role when she considers the verbal manifestations of the victim as contempt for authority, as we can see in the following examples.

Example (11)

57 58	Mary	no:oh, but listen, GIR↑L! ( ) I gave him a cow, girl (the cow's there) [ ]
59	Judge	oh, Joe (.) (the other one) can leave ( ) [ ]
60 61	Mary	the cow is there in the pasture look [ ]
62 63 64 65	Judge	>would you excuse me please< ( ) you talked, you didn't obey me, please... **if you keep on talking then I'm going to sto↑p, I'll arrest you for insubordination, okay**?
66 67	Mary	okay, but I gave two hundred reais from my retirement to pay ( )

Example (12)

311	Mary	but I don’t have any advantage [ ]
312 313 314 315		take a look here↓. I’ll warn you for the LAS↑T time >to you<. **if you keep on, <I’ll have to call the poLI↑ce> to arrest you, okay? I’ll call the poLI:ce to arrest every:body!**

Concluding Discussion

This study sought to investigate the roles enacted by a Judge in a Hearing of the Special Criminal Court in a city in the state of Minas Gerais, Brazil, based on Sarangi’s theoretical perspective (2000, 2010, 2011), concerning hybridity in institutional/professional settings. The analysis identified the following role-sets: professional roles, which refer to the accomplishment of the institutional mandate of the Hearing; pedagogic roles, marked by an orientation to the parties.

The professional role-set, including inquirer, mediator and expert, appears as required by the institutional mandate of the Criminal Hearing.

Regarding the pedagogical role-set enacted by the Judge, the role of educator becomes noticeable because the victim does not seem to be familiar with the systematics of turn-taking in this type of event (in this case, the judge is in charge of the allocation of turns of speaking and the selection of the topics). The role of police authority emerges when a participant cannot follow the conduct rules operating in this institutional interaction. The professional role of police authority as well as that of educator seemingly were selected by the Judge in order to strategically communicate all the conduct rules required in that specific context in a persuasive way. The pedagogic role of information provider becomes relevant through the perception of the judge indicating that the defendant cannot understand what must be done to abide by the sentence.

The professional roles of expert, inquirer and mediator help fulfil the mandate of institutional Criminal Hearings. They contribute to the clarification of the case being tried and help to investigate the facts and reconcile the litigants. These roles are required by institutional mandate of the Hearing and are directed towards the resolution of the case on trial. The other roles – police authority, advisor, educator and information provider – are not imposed by institutional mandate of this activity, but are interactional strategies chosen by the Judge for the referral of the resolution of the case.

Apparently, there is no conflict between the roles enacted by the Judge. On the contrary she was able to balance all the activity roles with the purpose of following and accomplishing the institutional agenda of the Hearing. Therefore role hybridity in the professional setting of Criminal Hearing may rather be considered in a complementary relation as it is closely linked to the creativity required to achieve the goals of the institutional mandate of this type of event.

References

Elliott, Philip 1972. *The Sociology of the Professions*. London: Macmillan.

Erickson, Frederick 1992. Ethnographic microanalysis of interaction. In Lecompte, M. / Millroy, W. / Preissle, J. (eds.) *The Handbook of Qualitative Research in Education*. New York: Academic: 201-226.

Foucault, Michel 1972. *The Archaeology of Knowledge*. New York: Pantheon Books.

Goffman, Erving [1959] 1985. *A Representação do Eu na Vida Cotidiana*. São Paulo: Vozes.

—. 1961. *Encounters: Two Studies in the Sociology of Interaction*. Indianapolis: Bobbs-Merrill.

Levinson, Stephen C. 1983. Conversational structure. In Levinson, S. C. *Pragmatics*. Cambridge: Cambridge University Press: 284-370.

Linton, Ralph [1945] 1971. The status-role concept. In Hollander, E. P. / Hunt, R. G. (eds.) *Classic Contributions to Social Psychology*. New York: Oxford University Press: 111-114.

Maynard, Douglas 1984. *Inside Plea Bargaining: The Language of Negotiation*. New York: Plenum.

Mehan, Hugh 1983. The role of language and the language of role in institutional decision making. *Language in Society* 12(2): 187-211.

Merton, Robert 1968. *Social Theory and Social Structure*. New York: Free Press.

Sacks, Harvey / Schegloff, Emanuel A. / Jefferson, Gail 1974. A simplest systematics for the organization of turn-taking for conversation. *Language* 50: 696-735.

Sarangi, Srikant 2000. Activity types, discourse types and interactional hybridity: the case of genetic counselling. In Sarangi, S. / Coulthard, M. (eds.) *Discourse and Social Life*. London: Pearson: 1-27.

—. 2010. Reconfiguring self / identity / status / role: the case of professional role performance in healthcare encounters. *Journal of Applied Linguistics and Professional Practice* 7(1): 75-95.

—. 2011. Role hybridity in professional practice. In Sarangi, S. / Polese, V. / Caliendo, G. (eds.) *Genre(s) on the Move: Hybridisation and Discourse Change in Specialised Communication.* Napoli: Edizioni Scientifiche Italiane (ESI): 271-296.

Sarangi, Srikant / Roberts, Celia (eds.) 1999. *Talk, Work and Institutional Order: Discourse in Medical, Mediation and Management Settings.* Berlin: Mouton de Gruyter.

Silveira, Sonia B. 2007. Uma perspectiva interacional em linguística. In Vasconcellos, Z. / Augusto, M. R. A. / Shepherd, T. M. G. (eds.) *Linguagem, Teoria, Análise e Aplicações.* Rio de Janeiro: Letra Capital: 8-17.

Strong, Philip M. / Davis, Alan G. 1978. Who's who in paediatric encounters: morality, expertise and the generation of identity and action in medical settings. In Davis, A. G. (ed.) *Relationships between Doctors and Patients.* Farnborough: Saxton House: 48-75.

Tannen, Deborah / Wallat, Cynthia 2002. Enquadres interativos e esquemas de conhecimento em interação: exemplos de um exame/consulta médica. In Ribeiro, B. T. / Garcez, P. M. (eds.). *Sociolinguística Interacional.* São Paulo: Loyola: 183-214.

CONTRIBUTORS

Paola Bocale is a Doctoral Researcher at the University of Cambridge, UK. She holds a PhD in Comparative Philology from 'La Sapienza' University in Rome and Masters' Degrees from the University of Cambridge and ARU. Her research interests include critical discourse analysis, linguistic ethnography, negotiation of identities in multilingual contexts and education of linguistic minority students. She is currently working on a project that explores the dynamics of ethno-linguistic identification in an Italian heritage community in the Crimea. Her most recent publications include articles on the linguistic practices of migrant communities in Italy and the UK and a monograph on the category of gender in the Slavic languages. Paola has a long time interest in restorative justice and has volunteered in restorative justice programmes in prisons for juveniles in the UK.

Ruth Breeze is Head of the Institute of Modern Languages at the University of Navarra, and a member of the GradUN Research Group in the *Instituto Cultura y Sociedad.* She has researched and published widely in the area of discourse analysis applied to media language and specialised discourse, focusing particularly on the field of legal English. Her most recent books are *Corporate Discourse* (Bloomsbury Academic 2013) and *Rethinking Academic Writing Pedagogy for the European University* (Rodopi 2012).

Stanisław Goźdź-Roszkowski is Associate Professor in the Department of Translation Studies, University of Łódź. His academic interests include legal linguistics and translation, corpus linguistics and phraseology. In particular, his recent research focuses on corpus-based and corpus-assisted analysis of evaluation in institutional discourse. He has published widely in the field of legal language and phraseology. He is the author of a book *Patterns of Linguistic Variation in American Legal English. A Corpus-based Study*. He is advisory board member for several journals in the fields of translation, corpus linguistics and discourse. He is on the editorial board of the *International Journal of Law, Language and Discourse*. He works as a freelance translator and expert witness for the Lodz local courts.

Bronwen Hughes holds a PhD in Linguistics and Modern and Comparative Literature (European School for Advanced Studies). She has extensively worked as a mother tongue language teacher at the University of Naples 'L'Orientale'. Currently, she also works as a contracted professor at the University of Suor Orsola Benincasa (Naples), where she teaches English for Tourism and National Heritage, as well as the University of Sannio where she teaches legal English. Her research interests lie in the fields of translation as a tool for second language acquisition, cross-cultural media studies, and forensic linguistics. In addition to a recently published research monograph *Investigating Format: A Conversation Analytical Study of the Interview Room Scenes in* The Bill *and* La Squadra (2009), she has also published research articles appearing in collected volumes.

Antonella Napolitano is a Researcher at the University of Sannio in Benevento. Before working full-time at university, she extensively taught at high school and was involved in several innovative language projects. Over the years her research has focused on institutional discourse with particular reference to the area of the European Community. She has also worked in the field of ESP and the language of advertising. Her recent work has centred on identity construction and gender studies as well as legal English. She has published widely in all the above-mentioned areas.

Stefano Ondelli is a Researcher in Italian at the Dipartimento di Scienze Giuridiche, del Linguaggio, dell'Interpretazione e della Traduzione of the University of Trieste. His main research interests concern sociolinguistic variation in modern Italian, Italian for special purposes (the language of interpreters and translators, legal and bureaucratic Italian, the language used in European Union institutions, the language of the press), Italian as a foreign language, corpus and quantitative linguistics and issues related to argumentative and technical writing.

Anna Franca Plastina is tenured Researcher in English Language and Translation at the University of Calabria (Italy), where she is also board member of the doctoral programme in Languages for Special Purposes and teaches ESP at the postgraduate school in Clinical Pathology. Her research interests lie mainly in Discourse Analysis, Psycholinguistics and ESP applied to Computer-Mediated Communication and Multimodality. Her most recent publications include: 'Multimodality in English for Specific Purposes: Reconceptualizing Meaning-making Practices', *Revista de Lenguas para Fines Específicos* (2013); 'Mashing Up the Web for

Academic Needs: A Study on Interdiscursivity and Genre Colonization' (2013); *Applied Linguistics and Semantic Web Apps: Cases of Mediated Discursive Practices* (2012); 'Tourism Destination Image: Distortion or Promotion? An Analysis of Web-based Promotional Discourse about Calabria' (2012).

Gianluca Pontrandolfo is a Research and Teaching Assistant at the University of Trieste (IUSLIT, Department of Legal, Language, Interpreting and Translation Studies) where he teaches general and specialised translation from Spanish into Italian. He combines his activity as free-lance translator with his academic and research interests. He has recently completed his PhD in Interpreting and Translation Studies (IUSLIT, University of Trieste) with a thesis focusing on a translation-oriented contrastive study of phraseological patterns in Spanish, Italian and English criminal judgments. His research interests include legal terminology/phraseology, corpus linguistics, translated vs. non-translated legal language, specialised genre studies and text linguistics.

Tarja Salmi-Tolonen LL.D., Phil.Lic., is Research Fellow at the Faculty of Law, University of Turku, Finland. She has lectured and conducted research on law and language at several universities in Finland and been invited to speak at US and European universities. She has worked at Cambridge University, UK, as a visiting scholar. She has been a member of several international research and curriculum development projects on language and law and an expert member of the language department of the Finnish Prime Minister's office and an invited speaker on law and language at government departments and district and appeal courts in Finland. She also acts as a referee for academic publications. Selected publications: 'Legal Linguistics as a Line of Study and an Academic Discipline' (in C. Williams and G. Tessuto 2013), 'A Contract is a Speech Act' (in Finnish in Haapio and Sipilä 2013), Language and the Functions of Law (2008), 'Persuasion in Judicial Argumentation' (in Halmari and Virtanen 2003).

Amitza Torres Vieira has a PhD in Language Studies from *Pontifícia Universidade Católica* of Rio de Janeiro, Brazil, and is an Adjunct Professor at *Universidade Federal de Juiz de Fora*, Brazil, at the Language Undergraduate course and the Linguistics Graduate Program. Her study interests include interaction, argumentation and evaluation in conflict situations, taking part in research projects that aim to describe and explain social and discursive practices in two institutional contexts: hearings in the Special Criminal Court and preliminary hearings at

PROCON (a Brazilian bureau of consumer protection linked to government administration). Her most recent publications are: 'Hibridismo de papéis na fala de uma Juíza do Juizado Especial Criminal' (Vieira e Marques, 2013) and 'A prática de avaliação no contexto de mediação familiar judicial' (Gago, Vieira e Santana, 2012).

Judith Turnbull is a foreign-language assistant at the Faculty of Economics, 'Sapienza' University of Rome. Her research interests include discourse analysis applied to the fields of economics and law and cross-cultural communication, with a particular focus on websites. Her recent publications include: 'Building, Enhancing and Defending Reputation in a Corporate Website, 2013, in *Space, Time and the Construction of Identity*, R. Salvi and J. Bowker (ed.), Peter Lang, 'For the reasons above, I consider that the Court should …': A linguistic analysis of argumentation in the opinions of British and Italian Advocates-General at the Court of the European Union', 2013, in *Language in the Negotiation of Justice*, C. Williams and G. Tessuto (eds.), Ashgate, and 'The blogs of the European Commission: public-private space in a professional institutional context', 2013, *Textus* XXVI (1).

INDEX